Dare to Walk in My Shoes

Confessions of a Sole Queen

by Nicole Jones

Sensual Steps Inc.

Chicago, Illinois

ISBN: 9780615319179
LCCN: 2009909279

Edited by Lissa Woodson and Patricia Boer
for Macro Marketing & Promotions Group
Interior Book Design by Lissa Woodson for www.macrompg.com
Cover Photograph and Cover Design by
Scot Scott for www.Biohertz.com

DEDICATION

This book is dedicated to my wonderful sister Jeanette Johnson, lovingly and affectionately known as "Netty." I know that you are looking down from heaven watching over our family with your warm heart. Thanks for being a wonderful big sister and always believing in me. I know that you are proud of me.

I love you always.

ACKNOWLEDGMENTS

The highest and ultimate praise to the Lord, for he hath given me the breath to live day to day. Through God's inspiration and love I am able to conquer all things. A special thanks to my Father, Samuel Johnson, who is my strength and my mother, Emma Jean Johnson, for her support. They have been married for 51 years and I am grateful to still have them in my life. Much love to Tiffany Hill and Janine Ingram my two dear friends who have supported my vision and mission without any doubts and have stood by my side through all trials and triumphs. Special thanks to Matthew, Maleiya, Mckinley and Johnathan Jones. Thank you to Mr. Buck and Tammy Williams-Blakely for believing in me and providing financial support. The Wheatly Family for their continuous love and support.

I would like to thank my brothers and sisters for being great siblings (Bryant, Greg, Audrey, Vanessa and my two step-brothers Maurice and Stevie Johnson), a host of nieces and nephews (Keyanna, Nathan, Martine, Tremaine, Kiara, Steven, Cara, James, George (my wonderful nephew), Sam, Dante, Therra, Tajj, Teri) April and Darnell Harris, Cassandra and Marcus Carr, Carla and James Robinson, Deborah and Kenny Gary, Cara and Danny Wilmington, Patrice Mallory, Ladonna Flanagan, Audrey Summerville, Michael Fayoyin, Michelle Mason, Pamela, Ameer and Anita Perkins, Rhea Henderson, Triniere Poole, Jorian Seay, Brittany Wright, Tracy Brigham, Alexandria Holmes, Jessica McDonald, Marilyn Gilbert, Louis James (Dominique), Terrell Shelton, Morris Brent, Traci Barnes,

Sister Sarah Martin, Johnathan and Jacinta Banks for their prayers, Anissa Braxton, Laurie Ogden-Powell, Mirion Green, Eboni McDonald, Tammy Davis, Alicia August-Wright, Roy Smith, Landis and Dominga (Mi-Spa and Landis has been doing my make-up since I was 14 years old), Sharon Williams, Yvette Clinton and many other close associates. Godchildren – Diamond, Ebony, Asia Ingram, Quo Vadis Gates and Paki Williams for reminding me to embrace my child like qualities.

I greatly appreciate the love of my aunts (Nancy, Ruth, Sarah, Carrie, Dorothy, Cora, Alice, and Earlene); and uncles (Genie, Clemon, and Carl). Gale and Dustin Cameron, Darryl, Tony, Sherron, Pierre, Wanda S., Deborah, Boaz, Keith, Ronnie, Susan, Betty, Diane, Wanda Crump, Latoya, Pumpkin and all of my many wonderful cousins. (As you can see I have a big family on both sides. It would take too much space to say everyone's name, but please realize I love you all the same.)

Special thanks to Lissa Woodson of Macro Marketing & Promotions Group for providing consultant assistance with starting my own publishing house and assisting me in the development and completion of this great book. Thanks to Johnathan Swain of Kimbark Beverages in Hyde Park, Patricia Boer, Naleighna Kai, Scot Scott of Biohertz, Frankie Payne of Genesis Printing & Copy Services, Malik Yusef and Buns, staff of Greater Auburn Gresham Development Corporation, Dedry Jones of the Music Experience, Robb Jackson of Soul Cafe, Desiree of Afrocentric Bookstore, DJ Jermaine, Cortez Carter, Dave Thomas of Luichiny (my favorite shoe design company), the Bridge Team, Mr. Cleveland McCowan, Greg and Shelia Barber, Father Michael Pfleger, Zondra Hughes, N'digo Magazine, my Pastor and his wife Bishop Horace Smith and

Sister Susan Smith, members of Apostolic Faith Church, Pastor Chris Harris and the Brightstar Church of God in Christ who has supported me for years, Pastor John Hannah of New Life Covenant Church, Pastor Terrance and Sister Lilanga Wallance.

It is definitely in order for me to thank many of the organizations and people who helped me realize my dreams: Lema Korshid, my attorney and now close associate, Alderman Toni Preckwinkle, Alderman Pat Dowell, Bernita Gabriel and the staff of Quad Community Development Corporation, Chicago Community Ventures (especially Christyn), Women's Business Development Center (www.wbdc.org), Elizabeth Gardner, Ericka King, Hedy Ratner, Sylvia Wynn, and Teresa Prim. Cheryl Jackson, CEO of The Chicago Urban League, Gus Tucker, The William J. Clinton Foundation, Kwame Raoul;s Office, Oreal, True Star Magazine – Nae Tae, Deanna Grant – Accountant, Jack Crane, former Vice President (who helped me complete my first rehab project), Greg Johnson, Marcia Nichols at Shorebank. Thomas Cole and Matthew Gambs from Diamond Bank for helping a new opportunity flourish for me. To the many wonderful Bronzeville Businesses located in our rising neighborhood (Faie African Art, My Secret Place, Fort Smith, Bronzeville Coffee House, Little Black Pearl, Room 43, Agriculture, Z & H, Ain't She Sweet and all interns who work with me at Sensual Steps Shoe Salon. Deborah Brown, who exposed me to multiple news and media opportunities. All of the entrepreneurs that I partner with on a continuous basis, but especially Kiwi Boutique, Krazy Kake House, Authenticity Board Game, Chatham Theaters, Wendell Granville of Mama Pickeys Chocolate, Toni Fleming of Sassi Soles, and many, many more who are a big part of building and developing our businesses. To the ladies taking my POP (Power of Prosperity) class; supporters of my business who have been amazing: Kimberly Hollingsworth, Sharon Williams, Ramonski Luv and Joe Soto, Bionce Foxx, Herb Kent and his wonderful finance Linda, Nikki Woods, Ken Bedford, and Errol Dunlap (InChiCity).

P.U.M.P.S. (Providing U Motivation to Pursue Success), the non-for profit organization I founded to help build self-esteem, self image and teach teenage girls about conflict resolution (www.pumpsuccess.com) all of the girls that stuck out the program and all of our wonderful Board Member and volunteers.

To Keith 1, Keith 2 and Mr. Jones, the three men who have provided many lessons in life that have helped me develop into a secure, loving, well-groomed woman seeking a lifetime filled with opportunity. I'm glad that all of you have matured and become exceptional men.

I would be remiss if I didn't thank all of my clients who have supported me throughout the years and share the same shoe passion. It is because of the support of you I am able to tell this story!

"There are two mistakes one can make along the road to truth...not going all the way, and not starting."

---Prince Gautama Siddharta

"Three things cannot be long hidden: the sun, the moon, and the truth."

---Prince Gautama Siddharta

From My Heart to Yours ....

The oversized gold-framed mirror installed in the shoe salon was a major part of a pink, bubble gum fantasy. I wanted my clientele to look in that mirror and reconnect with their childhood; wanted the women who strolled into the store to feel pampered and pretty. Like princesses.

However, there were many days when I looked in the mirror and saw the "ugly" unspoken truth in its reflection. When my clients and staff looked at me they saw a successful businesswoman. They saw a friend. They saw a smile—always. But I could never fool the mirror. My smile didn't quite reach my eyes any more. How could it? The business was losing money faster than high heels could break under pressure. My real estate investments were costing more money than they gained. The strain of trying to maintain appearances was slowly sucking the life out of my marriage.

The mirror knew it all.

When I reached the lowest point … the point of no return, the point of not giving a damn anymore, something wonderful happened. *Vision.*

From this vision I was able to cut losses, refocus my life's strategy and build a circle of power that could set everything back on track. From this vision I gathered the strength and discipline to turn it all around. No longer am I just looking the part of a successful woman—I am now living it. Thanks to a few key changes in my life, the mirror now holds a truer image than ever before—an image of one of God's chosen women.

I invite you to take a walk in my shoes, get a glimpse of my life—the mistakes, the indecisions and most of all, the triumphs. It is my hope that by the end of this book you, too, will be standing tall on a solid life strategy that will revolutionize your personal outlook and re-energize your entrepreneurial spirit.

Are you with me? Alright then.

Let's step!

"All that we are is the result of what we have thought. The mind is everything. What we think we become."

---Prince Gautama Siddharta

CHAPTER 1
MARY JANES
TAKING THOSE BABY STEPS

Allow me, for a moment, to take the time to recall this most painful chapter of my life. Entrepreneurship involves intimacy, clarity and honesty—and I plan to give it to you straight, no chaser.

Entering the business world with true understanding of self is vital because *You* are the foundation of your business, of your empire. Empires built upon shaky foundations or with unknown substances are destined to collapse.

Some have asked why I decided to open a shoe salon. What lies behind this passion for pumps? On the one foot, I have a shoe fetish that I want to share with the world, and on the other, a passion for pampering and empowering women. I want to adorn their feet with fancy shoes. What many don't realize is this passion, this love, is the result of several painful experiences in my own life.

Consider this: when standing tall, shoes are the furthest things from the natural eye. Though the eyes are the windows to the soul, there are ways to draw attention away from the place where everyone seems to first look. The prettier the shoes, the less likely one is to focus on the eyes—and especially the secrets, pain, disappointment or hurt that may dwell behind them. Herein lies where my story begins and the truth unfolds.

I grew up on the South Side of Chicago—in Auburn-Greshman, not too far from the Englewood area. I'm extremely grateful that I lived in a two-parent home as it allowed me the opportunity to witness what love could be like between two individuals. It also gave me the ability to see the trials and tribulations that relationships experience. Through it all, for the love of their six children, my parents were able to press through and provide a decent life for us.

My father, the backbone of the Johnson family, only had a third grade education. It's so funny looking back, because I never realized this important fact until I was in my early twenties. My father made sure that we were everywhere the name of Jesus was mentioned: Wednesday night Bible study, Thursday Bible class at home, Friday choir practice at church—even though I couldn't sing a lick——and Sunday we would be at every church service. When I saw my father in any educational capacity, it was with his Bible in hand. Listening to him read from any one of those sixty-six books, naturally he stumbled over many of the words, but then so did I and a few others. For that reason, I believed his way of reading the Bible was normal.

My mother graduated from high school and went on to become a cashier, so there wasn't a very heavy emphasis on education in my household. My father, on the other hand, was very adamant in making sure that I, as well as my five siblings, understood what entrepreneurship was all about. In more ways than one, that was a blessing in my life; though I will tell anyone that having both—education and drive to become an entrepreneur—is key to achieving immeasurable success.

My father, even with only a third grade education, owned multiple businesses: a limousine company that rented cars to funeral homes and for special occasions; a liquor store; record store and many other small businesses. It amazes me, even to this day, that my father could not read, but one thing he could do was count and keep up with his money. When I was about twelve years old, he told me that as a young Black woman I may find it hard in life to work for other people; that at some point they would be in control of how much money I made and how far I could go. He told me that I needed to be an "entroproknow," (yes, he said it exactly that way).

At Clara Barton Elementary School, Mrs. Latham, my 5th grade teacher, asked what I wanted to be when I grew up, I proudly said I wanted to be an "entroproknow like my Dad." She immediately corrected me, then explained exactly what the word meant and how to properly use it. Fortunately, she didn't discourage me, as so many others do when children aspire to do something outside of the norm. At that time, black people landed in jobs that ranged from teachers, nurses, police officers, bankers, with only a few becoming doctors, lawyers, and journalists. No one else in my class desired to achieve the same goals as I did. Somehow it didn't deter me or make me feel ashamed of my choice. If my father could do it, then so could I, a little black girl from the South Side of Chicago.

Though my father worked many hours a day away from home, when he was in our presence, he was always talking about what he did for a living. He loved all of his jobs; loved being his own boss. I soaked up his love for that kind of freedom, as though they were my daily lessons. My siblings eventually went into fields that were as far away from being business owners as possible. I think my father's zeal, his drive for business, rubbed off on me with every conversation; with every question he answered——and I had many.

My mother, however, was the total opposite of my father. She simply wanted to be comfortable and didn't desire anything outside of a small home and reliable transportation. There was total greatness inside of my mother, but she let life drag her along and missed out on the opportunity to achieve her higher calling. Although she supported my dad to a degree, it was with great skepticism. He did not let her attitude towards his endeavors discourage him. He was able to provide for his wife, all six children, and even his children from a previous marriage.

My father was a very frugal man. He didn't believe in wasting money or resources. We were his "human" resources—especially since he put food on the table, clothes on our backs, and a roof over our heads. Each one of his children spent time working in his business in one capacity or another. I like to say that we were little "Jamaicans," (three job mon!), which is not a slight in any way as Jamaicans are known to be hard-working and enterprising. The job I hated the most was the limousine service. When the cars were dirty, we had to wash them and make sure they were sparkling clean. That was fine for summer, but as everyone knows, Chicago winters can be brutal. We were out in below zero temperatures, washing, drying, shining, waxing or whatever. It's no wonder that I have a great love for warm clothing, forced air heating, and a sheer love for furry boots.

Our jobs outside of the home did not overshadow what we were required to do in the kitchen, bathrooms and garden in the little Cape Cod house on Seeley Avenue. I can remember once being awakened at one o'clock in the morning with my father yelling at the top of his lungs. When he would yell, I was instantly like a soldier standing at attention because it was usually butt-whipping time. All I could think was, "Jesus, what did we do wrong this time?" He woke everyone in the house, made us come downstairs, and line up in front of his bed, before pointing to the mussed covers. "Why didn't y'all make up my bed?" Something so simple, but it mattered to him. Especially since my mother was pulling the late night shift as a cashier. All six of us got a little whipping that morning before being sent back to bed. Trust me, his bed was made every day after that. Chores around the house—painting the garage, gardening, doing the dishes, laundry, cooking (at age twelve for me which I didn't perfect until I was thirty-four), were taken as seriously as the jobs we had working for our dad. Slacking was strictly prohibited in either case. And I certainly took him and any responsibilities I was given very seriously. Maybe too seriously. I stopped eating cereal and playing with dolls at nine years old. I thought both were childish, and in no way did I want to be considered a child—especially since I aspired to be an "entropronow" just like my dad.

During my childhood days my world revolved around the community and the community was centered around the church. Everyone loved my father. He was serious, business-oriented, hardworking, funny, reliable, honest and trustworthy—but he didn't play. The few times he did smile were from jokes that he told himself or from being around his family, including his sisters and brothers. I learned a great deal from him—he exposed me to God, exposed me to the world of managing and owning a business, but there was one thing missing. He never really showed me that he loved me. I longed for him to hug me, to tell me that I was daddy's little girl, because this is what I saw happening with the other children who lived near us when they interacted with their fathers. I learned later in life that my father's parents weren't very affectionate. He couldn't do something for me that hadn't been shown or given to him. Wanting and desiring to feel special in the eyes of my father led to me making many mistakes in life when it came to men. This resulted in painful moments in my childhood and experiences during my teen years whose weight carried well into my adult years.

In high school, I was a different type of young lady. I entered into a long-term relationship at a very early age—fifteen. My boyfriend at the time was raised in a Catholic household with a strict upbringing. His parents were not receptive to "outsiders," but I made it into their tight circle for a while. Unfortunately, that soon changed when his parents could no longer stand the sight of me. In their eyes, I was taking their young boy and making him into a man way too soon. This was heartbreaking as a teenager, but I later learned that teenagers often mistake lust for love which could lead to many pains and problems in their future.

My boyfriend and I dated until I turned twenty-one. Being in a relationship at such an early age, I gravitated and clung to what I thought was love, because I was trying to fill that void my father had left. At least I perceived it to be a void. Unlike some households, at least my dad was there and provided for us, but a great deal of the time I missed him because of the long hours spent away from home. I would later learn that "time" is just one of the sacrifices that are made when you decide to be an entrepreneur.

When you are trying to find love, you will mistake anything for that coveted interaction. I mistook infatuation for love. I can say now that being in a "serious" relationship at such an early age is detrimental to the mental health of a young woman. It becomes a distraction from educational goals and from getting to the next level in life. It's a hindrance to developing healthy relationships with others since everything, every action becomes filtered through the eyes of that other person. Instead of relying on one's inner voice, the spirit of God that dwells in each one of us, approval is sought from that other person before moving in a direction that one knows is right.

Like so many teenagers who had walked into "love," I began to lose my identity. Many things have been put in place to ensure that young men and women have the boundaries and a frame of character reference to draw from: the Bible, church, sports, dance and reading. Regrettably, I stepped totally outside of those things—trying to be my own "little woman." That in itself was one of the biggest mistakes I could have ever made. Having control over one's own person, one's life, is the key to a strong foundation.

When I was in high school, for some apparent reason, I thought I was a business woman. I carried a briefcase instead of a book bag, wore heels instead of gym shoes, dressed in silk blouses and skirts instead of trousers and sweats. I was not the type of young lady to attend games or other school functions, because I thought they were childish. Although I was very popular in school and not the type of person to land in trouble, I just thought I was "grown." Looking back, I realize I missed out on a lot of fun things—things that would have shaped my experiences much differently. My actions stemmed from being in a relationship where I wanted to be taken seriously by this young man, wanting him to love and desire me and to separate myself from the image of other girls. I was an overachiever with above-average grades, but they would have been stellar if I wasn't trying to do things to impress "Mr. Man."

Some of the mistakes I made then affected my life years later. When I went away to college that first year, I plunged feet first into credit card debt traveling back and forth from Normal, Illinois, to Chicago every weekend to be with him. I had fourteen credit cards and four gas station cards (mind you, I didn't have a car). After two years in college they were all maxed out. Bill collectors were ringing the phone 24/7, I had to work to pay the credit cards and my grades started to slip. I gave up, ran back home to be with him, only to come home to a rude awakening. I lost my scholarship. I lost my integrity. I damn near lost my mind.

I practically made an ass of myself when I found out that I, the woman who gave up so much for "love," was merely a speck of female dust on his player radar. The weekend before Labor Day we stayed at one of his friend's houses for the weekend. We were asleep and their phone rang in the middle of the night. I assumed it was his friends calling to check on us. At least that's what I told him. Inwardly, unfortunately, something just didn't feel right. So I ran to answer the phone and a woman on the other end said a breathy, "Hello." I steeled myself because my mind let me know something was wrong, even though I answered with, "Hi, how are you? Who would you like to speak to?" When she said, "Keith" my heart fell down to my toes. I couldn't reel in my emotions so I screamed, "Who is this?" She simply said, "This is Jackie. Who are *you*?" As if she had a right to demand anything. I retorted, "Jackie who? And why are you calling here, at this house, for my man." Then she replied with the words that no woman wants to hear, "Baby, I was there with him yesterday."

I woke Keith. Too bad for Keith, I used the phone upside his head to accomplish that task. As he was frightened out of a sound sleep, I dropped that tiny bit of information about Jackie into his ear. He immediately started in with the lies and back-peddling. He said I was crazy, that he didn't know who that was and someone was trying to do him in. Lies—all of it. And the sad part about it is, I started to believe him anyway. I pictured the last six years, the times I blew off with friends and family; the times I put him before everyone, and the fact that I had loved him more than I loved myself, and sought his approval for things happening in my life. I thought of all this and realized

I had invested too much of myself and to walk away at this point would mean I did it all for nothing.

Although I knew I wouldn't go too far, I pretended that I was about to leave him—to force his hand on professing his love for me, to force some kind of reaction from him other than just the lies spewing from his lips. When I made it to the elevator, two ladies were getting off——one of them was three times my petite size, and the other was just my size. She looked at me and said, "You must be Nicky." I could only reply with, "You must be Jackie." She nodded, and I said, "Let's knock on this door and figure out what's going on."

When Keith pulled open the door and saw the three of us, he almost passed out. Then the fight began. She screamed at him. I screamed at him. And her friend put in her little two cents, too. I kept my eye on the big girl because she looked a lot like the terminator! While Jackie screamed at him—I was thinking survival too, wondering how I could take her down! Over all, it was not a pleasant undertaking. We woke everyone on that floor of that high rise building in South Shore.

Now here's the sad part: I was so bold at the time, and so filled with what I believed was love that I was going to fight for "my man." I grabbed the bat from a nearby closet and stormed toward the front door. The ladies weren't really trying to deal with anything going upside their heads so they swiftly moved toward the elevators. After I watched Jackie cry and cry and plead for him to be with her, he told her she was crazy and shut the door in her face. And somehow I thought I had won the prize. Little did I know, I had lost more than I gained. I was now an official card-carrying member of the low self-esteem club. This was merely the beginning of a roller coaster ride of painful relationships.

Teenage girls often find themselves in relationships at early ages seeking the love of a young man for all the love they are missing from home. Especially now, children are born to younger parents which means being raised in single parent homes without a true perception of what it takes to raise children. Teenage girls may not have their fathers in the household to educate them on how they should be treated by a young man. This often results in young ladies rushing into loveless relationships and believing that sexual intercourse is love.

I noticed in my high school years at Bogan Computer Tech, teens were coming up pregnant and the numbers of those teens increased greatly. I was always very shocked to see a teenage girl give up her freedom to be weighted down with a child. This was never an option for me even though I was in a serious relationship. I never believed that having a child by a man would keep him. In fact it does just the opposite—it pushes the young man away. He is still an adolescent ready to experience the world. The young man is simply seeking temporary enjoyment, not a life time commitment. His mind is not on building a family, changing diapers, paying bills, educating a child ...when he is simply a child himself.

This misconception of love brings about much hurt and pain for a generation of families when teenage girls become mothers before their time. I choose not to become a mother because it was simple mathematics to me: I observed that the teenagers who had children were dumped by those men immediately. The young men were on a hunt for the next young lady that he could enjoy a temporary moment of fulfillment without any responsibility. Attempting to force a permanent relationship with immature teenage boys caused them do despise the young women they impregnated. Most teenage mothers that I know never ended up with the man who got them pregnant.

All for the sake of what we believe is love, women may feel the consequences for the rest of their lives. But we can change the impact. We have control over our future. Beginning to find love inside of yourself is of great importance, then working on things that you love helps to alleviate the need for imaginary love from another person. A major key component to living a life that honors you and that others respect is to learn how to "Love thyself" and find out what you absolutely LOVE to do in life. People harbor passions that are hidden deep down in their souls. They awake from dreams about indulging in the opportunity to fulfill this desire only to lose the courage and somehow convince themselves that it was only a dream. I assure you that the dream can live if you breathe life into it. Whatever you desire to put your time and energy into can surely prosper. If you choose to seek love inside of other people, instead of finding love and passion for you and your desires, you could miss out on an infinite amount of possibilities that could lead to many disappointments in your future.

Think BIG…the world belongs to you. Let's stop making mistakes all for the sake of love and begin to find love in goals and dreams we secretly harbor. What do you really love to do? Embrace it and begin to learn everything about it become a subject matter expert and redirect your love.

Do you want to be an Entrepreneur?

Being an entrepreneur is not an idea that one pulls out of thin air. There must be a driving, passionate force of power which completely ignites your inner being. People who seek out becoming an entrepreneur strictly because they don't want to take orders from someone else, are doing it for the wrong reasons. Entrepreneurs are witty, strong-willed, determined and, most importantly, they must be in it for the long haul.

As a child I was attracted to my father's determination to succeed. I admired him more as a young adult when I realized he did it with only a third grade education. Before taking this step in life, know for sure exactly what you want to be and understand why. I worked hard and built a lot of knowledge prior to becoming a business owner. I had a zeal for setting my own schedule, creating my dream salary and building an empire in the community for everyone to enjoy. My initial thoughts of being an entrepreneur as a child, teenager and adult were all completely different than what I was actually faced with in the real world.

Wikipedia states that an entrepreneur is a person who has possession of an enterprise and venture and assumes significant accountability for the inherent risks and the outcome. It is an ambitious leader who combines land, labor and capital to often create and market new goods or services. Key words are stated here...*a person assuming risk and outcomes*. This is more than a person with a great vision. Know that entrepreneurship is the right direction for your life. Because the decision to build a business without the commitment can be a costly, timely and disappointing venture. Become an entrepreneur because it lives and breathes inside of you; because the desire fills every essence of you, and you are prepared to dedicate your life to that mission.

Chapter 1: Questions to Ask Yourself:

What is stopping you from stepping out of your comfort zone now to achieve the big dream that permeates in your thoughts daily?

Get out your journal and write out your thoughts.

Luke 6:47-48—Whoever comes to Me, and hears My sayings and does them, I will show you whom he is like: He is like a man building a house, who dug deep and laid the foundation on the rock. And when the flood arose, the stream beat vehemently against that house, and could not shake it, for it was founded on the rock.

"Your work is to discover your world and then with all your heart to give yourself to it."

---Prince Gautama Siddharta

CHAPTER 2
SLING BACKS

My father laid the foundation, but over time I acquired the taste and the drive to know what it was like to become my own boss. Then I learned there was another mistake my father made. He had not shared the wisdom of proper planning and saving money. He knew how to make it, but not how to save for a rainy day . . . or any day for that matter.

Let's do the math. My father had multiple business, didn't know how to save or plan ahead, had several mouths to feed and to provide for—so with everything coming in—there was much more going out. By most people's definition, we were still working-class poor. I felt I was destined to live a better quality of life—but the twenty thousand dollar debt I accumulated during those two years of college soon had me living in the style that I grew up in—and sometimes not even that.

Since I thought I was "grown" and no longer wanted advice from my parents, I had moved out and began to live in a means that was less than poor. Everything coming in was already designated to go right back out and none of it was used for the things I wanted to do. Like father, like daughter. I wish my family—or someone—would have told me the dangers of too much credit and not using it wisely. It would have prevented many years of financial hardship. I started in the negative rather than hitting the ground running from zero and going upward and onward from that point.

That twenty thousand dollars worth of debt felt like two hundred thousand. My ignorance forced me to take jobs that did not require a strong educational background and consisted of manual labor in some cases. I landed a job as 10-key punch operator at Northern Trust Bank—a Fortune 500 company. Trust me that "Fortune" didn't end up in my bank account. Let me explain what this job entailed. As people wrote out and deposited checks into their accounts, I was the one responsible for putting the little black numbers identifying what the dollar amount of the checks were.

The job was initially a temporary position, and I would have to prove myself to stay in a more permanent capacity. I worked from 5:00 a.m. to 8:00 a.m.—a mere three hours every day, which meant working two other jobs just to make ends meet. I was attracted to a higher standard of living—though I didn't have it growing up. I wanted the fancy cars, the designer suits, the money and power—things that seemed to command respect. One major reason I desired these things could be traced back to my self-esteem issues—the need for approval, the need for love, the need for someone or something outside of myself to say that I was of value. I felt that if I could look good on the outside, people would assume that everything on the inside mirrored one and the same.

At the age of twenty-one, when all my friends were graduating from college, embarking on those wonderful corporate careers, going on vacations and having a wonderful time, I was working my way out of debt and trying to regain my center. A manager at The Northern Trust Company (TNT), a man by the name of Greg Barber walked up to me one night and said, "You don't belong here. Why are you here?" Classic question. I looked at him and couldn't respond—because my mind went blank. He said, "take a look around." For the first time after a year of being in that place, I noticed my co-workers. All of them were middle-aged, mostly black women, with families—some with *grandchildren*—with very little income. But the thing that stood out the most was their faces and posture—sad and serious. Most of them were unhappy. This is where my life was headed.

That evening we engaged in a long conversation which I will never forget. Greg, having taken the time to point out the obvious, sparked fear in my soul. I didn't want to end up thirty years later still punching numbers on other people's checks. I didn't want to settle for less. It would be different if the women were happy and if this was a career of their choosing. For the most part, it was all they could do because of their education or lack thereof; it was also due to the fact that they didn't necessarily aspire to do more than collect a paycheck at a job that was far under their abilities. Nothing wrong with that if it makes you happy, but it wasn't for me—and I'm sure that given another opportunity—it really wasn't for them either.

Most women desire to do something different, something great—it is fear that keeps us stuck in places where we really don't want to be. It is lack of choices or fear of failure that stifles us. Those women, my co-workers, reminded me of my mother—the fact that she "tolerated" my father's aspirations. Sadly, deep in her heart, she had also settled. She worked as a cashier at a liquor store for several years until it closed. Minimum pay, and not many opportunities for advancement. She wasn't happy either.

This revelation and reflection proved to be an awakening for me. I got my butt back in school—pronto. Attending Malcolm X College, a community college, only added to my already hectic schedule, but living with the stigma of being a college dropout was not an option. Not one member of my immediate family had a college education and I wanted to be different. No one in my immediate family encouraged my desire to finish college—I had to cheer myself on and find a way to position myself around other positive influences.

Greg told me that since I was over twenty-one, investing my money would be the smart way to go. My question to him was, "What money?" I still hadn't cleared the debt by any stretch of the imagination. And like many around me, I was living paycheck to paycheck. There were days when even the bare necessities escaped my reach. But I didn't brush off his advice, either. I tucked it into a small corner of my mind knowing that the moment any extra money surfaced, I would invest it. In the meantime, I would learn what I could about investing.

Greg also inspired me to find a better job within the company. I was actually beginning to believe that the job I held was all I could have; that I had messed up so bad there was no way out. I soon learned a lesson about life and about God: there is always a window of opportunity waiting to be opened, waiting to pour in sunshine. Greg cracked open the window with just a few words that night—my drive and initiative did the rest. Even though my pennies could hardly be stretched, I took Greg's advice and begin investing the minimum of five percent immediately from my check. I knew that additional sacrifices would have to be made to help supplement this missing money so I began to sell jewelry on the side. Yes, I drove to Clark Street where there are a multitude of manufacturers to, purchased discounted jewelry, and begin my first entrepreneurial investment by reselling those goods at a higher price.

I also took a job in the vault to get off the night shift so I would be able to meet more people within corporate America. Lifting seventy-pound bags of other people's money meant I could at least rub up against what the rich folks took for granted every day—an unending supply of cash. The Northern Trust Company was the place where the ultra rich put their money . . . money in established trust funds, money in corporations and money in multi-million dollar empires. Thankfully, this job did not require that I dress professionally. Unlike my high school years of wearing business casual clothing and carrying a briefcase, I couldn't afford to buy a scarf, let alone a suit. Although I always snuck in a pair of cute, affordable shoes ... no matter what.

After three months of building my muscles by lifting those heavy bags, my back went out. I weighed a buck-o-five soaking wet and some of those bags were bigger than I was. Now I was caught in another dilemma—to find another job within the company in thirty days or I would have to leave altogether. By the grace of God a lady by the name of Islee Ferguson, who has since made her transition, provided me with an opportunity of a lifetime. Though I had no experience in that area, she offered the opportunity for a client service position, which is as far from vault work as one could get. On the day of the interview, I had purchased a red dress from the thrift store and walked in with that old high school briefcase to add to the "look" and "feel" of why I should qualify for the position. Little did I know, red was probably not the best color to wear in a banking environment—especially since it was layered on a dress that hugged every curve I had (and ones I didn't know about). Fortunately, Islee saw past the dress, but lovingly suggested that I invest in "other clothes."

When Mrs. Ferguson asked about my work experience during the interview, I thought that honesty was the best policy. I answered her with a simple, "Ms. Ferguson, everyone else that you might interview can walk in this door and tell you that they've had years of experience servicing clients. I cannot."

She took a deep breath, but I continued with, "However, the one thing that is important, is that they know how to do it *their* way, and I'm going to do it *exactly* the way you teach me, with a fresh start and with no preconceived notions about how it should be done. That in itself gives me a competitive edge."

Needless to say, she loved my tenacity and agreed to try me out. This was nothing short of a miracle . . . at least in my eyes! As a client service associate, I would do every single thing it took to learn every aspect of the banking business. I brought the prospectus home and studied it as well as the scriptures my father had made us study in the Bible. I tried my best to know the answers to questions that investors would even *think* to ask. I arrived early every day and stayed way past closing time. Any time they needed someone to work overtime, I was their woman! I became known as someone who was dependable, trustworthy, honest and went above and beyond the call of duty. Sounds familiar? Like father, like daughter.

Over time, I inspired other employees with motivational and encouraging words. Strangely enough, I ended up teaching people who had been there for years things about the business that they never took the time to read or comprehend. This was about the time I noticed that some people didn't value their jobs or the opportunities they had been given—and it was a shame. There I was, coming from a position where I punched numbers on checks, then to a point of back-breaking work inside the vault, then to a position that exposed me to a variety of people requiring the use of perception, brains and tenacity—and it was taken for granted by some of those around me.

After one year in that position, I received a nice-sized raise—which I certainly appreciated. Then a very confusing situation occurred shortly thereafter. A workflow coordinator's position became available, and I just knew that job was for me. I *knew* Mrs. Ferguson was going to give that job to me, especially since I was practically handling all aspects of the position anyway. I was brought into a meeting with the certainty that the position was all but mine. To my surprise, each person in my unit was being introduced to our "new" workflow coordinator—someone who didn't have a stitch of experience! Now how did that happen? I worked my sling back pumps off (and a few other things, too), and this man, dressed in a suit (with fine-looking shoes I might add), comes walking in and just takes *my* position. I was completely dismayed. Where did he come from? And what made them think he was better suited for the position?

A few days later, I built up the courage to walk into Mrs. Ferguson's office and asked for a meeting. Through my tears I managed to ask, "How could you do this to me?" Looking back, I realize I was much too emotional. However, this beautiful, dark-skinned, robust woman looked at me as if to say, "Do what?" And if I remember correctly she did say those words. I dried my tears before continuing with, "How could you let that man take *my* job? I have worked my toes to the nub."

She leaned back in her big black office chair. "Nicole, yes. You would deserve this job, but when were you going to tell me that's what you wanted to do? Am I supposed to *guess* that you want to be a manager? During your performance appraisals, did you mention your career goals? Or your desire to go into management?" She leaned forward, looking me straight in the eyes as her voice became solid and steady, "If you want something in life, you'd better learn to ask for it." I didn't blink an eye as her meaning carried. I dried what was left of my tears, squared my shoulders and in the strongest voice I could manage, said, "I want to go into management. Now what do I need to do to get there?" She smiled at me and answered with a simple, "Keep doing what you're doing."

I continued to work even harder. Two months later, a team leader position became available—one that was above the work flow coordinator. The job was handed to me in a silver slipper—with a nice raise, too! The woman didn't have to tell me twice! Ask and it shall be given. Another lesson learned from just one of the wonderful people I met on my life's journey. Just to think that I was disappointed about not getting the other position when God had already set up soemthing so much better!

Chapter 2: Questions to Ask Yourself

If being an entrepreneur is what you've decided, let's talk about your passion: what do you absolutely love to do and why?

Write your thoughts in your journal.

Romans 8:28—And we know that all things work together for good to those who love God, to those who are the called according to His purpose.

CHAPTER 3
LOAFERS

The Northern Trust Company position was working out fine, but because I still had a mountain of debt to climb out of, I also worked another job as a leasing agent. This time in my life reminded me a great deal of my childhood days when I, along with my siblings, worked at several of my father's businesses. Same work ethic, different time.

As a leasing agent, I had the opportunity to meet another person who would make a dynamic impact on my life. Lessons learned while listening to Greg Barber at TNT would come into play during my time at the leasing office.

Greg had already encouraged me to invest five percent of my paycheck into stocks. For a number of reasons I felt I could not afford to do it. I barely had anything to buy food once all my bills were paid, but he said I couldn't afford *not* to do it. I decided to take him on his challenge and found a way to invest something out of every check. The amounts were so small that when I received the quarterly statements, I just filed them away. After about a year, I noticed the amount of funds I had available had actually doubled! My first inclination was to withdraw it all, baby! Instead I increased the amount of money I was investing from five percent to eight percent. Now even more sacrifices had to be made on the home front, such as visits to the hair stylist only taking place once a month. Eventually, I ended up doing my own hair, nails and I went on a complete strike from clothes and jewelry shopping. However, I would treat myself to one thing on occasion—shoes to accent my wardrobe, to liven things up—but no other luxuries were allowed.

Buckling down also meant that eating out was completely out of the question. Unfortunately, at the time I didn't know how to cook that well. Though my father taught me how to cook some things, I ended up buying and stocking up on canned goods to take up the slack. This was a very humbling experience for me. As my investments continued to grow, I wasn't hurting or upset (though I did get sick of the food I could actually cook, like spaghetti). I was happy to make sacrifices that would make my life better.

There are certain things I have considered to be my greatest attributes—having an open mind and the willingness to listen and learn, especially from people who have demonstrated great leadership. I believe you can learn something from anyone; even if it's how you *don't* want to be like that person or mirror their actions. For instance, I used to work out in the gym every morning at TNT. But even after leaving the gym, I would scarf down a Snickers bar, which was counterproductive.

When I first started working out, there was this fine, well-built trainer with blonde hair and blue eyes (did I mention he was fine? F*oine!*) His body was off the chain! Studying him, examining how he did things, led me to believe that he was a prime example of leadership when it came to working out. He shared success techniques, his eating habits and all the essential things that I needed to know to build my body up.

He left the company a couple of years later and was replaced by a beautiful, friendly, wonderful young woman. Unfortunately, she didn't practice any of the things she tried to teach. By comparison to my previous trainer, this woman was shorter than my 5'5" frame and over two hundred pounds. Her appearance and lack of discipline soon resulted in my inability to work out with her. Not that I was judging her harshly, but I, like so many others, expect a leader to lead by example. She and I had something in common after all: we both loved Snickers bars. Nevertheless, if you're going to teach people, you should learn and apply it to your own life first. For example, Greg Barber knew how and what to do with investing into the stock market. Greg's sound advice would help me in my next financial undertaking, but it was the example from the young female trainer who would make me take a long, hard look at my values in my personal life. That's a story for a little later.

Cleveland McCowan, property manager for a new development project in Chicago, introduced me to the wonderful world of real estate right in the community where I currently reside. Everything came full circle, I'm back in the booming Bronzeville area. Not only did Cleveland introduce me into the real estate world, he taught me how to be a great business woman. Although I didn't have any leasing experience when I applied for the job, I used my famous line——the same one that landed me the customer service position at TNT: *Hey they already know what to do, but I'm going to do it the way you teach me—and to perfection.*

Now I was twenty-two years old, had been investing for one year and was still living check to check. I would, ultimately, carve a way out. As I listened to and mirrored other successful people, I was able to learn and grow beyond measure. Cleveland told me something that I thought was a joke at first.

"Nicole, you need to acquire some money and invest it into a piece of property."

What would make him think that I could afford to buy a property? I posed that question to him and he responded with something I'll never forget: "What makes you think you can't?"

I have noticed that intelligent people always have quick responses. They tend to answer a question with a question in a way that forces you to think. I rattled off quite a few reasons that came to mind, "I'm broke. I don't have any money right now. I'm trying to get myself out of debt."

Cleveland said, "Okay. You've told me about some of the barriers. Fair enough. Now tell me how you're going to get *beyond* the barriers, because you can't let them stop you from reaching success or obtaining a goal." I pondered those words for a moment before saying, "Teach me! Teach me what I need to know, and if I think this is something I can do, I'll do it."

Wow! I remember like it was yesterday—being so inspired by those simple, thought-provoking words that came from his mouth, and the even more powerful ones that followed. Mainly, the gist of it was, if I bought a building, I could actually begin to live rent free. Cleveland showed me on paper how it was done. He broke down the costs of a mortgage on a two flat, rent that I could collect and other ways to make money from the building. He showed me that instead of paying so much in taxes, I could actually recoup more funds per year. Right off the bat, he made me understand everything about the numbers in real estate that would help to make changes in my finances.

Everything he said made sense to me, but deep down inside I wasn't sure if I could do it. The more I listened to him the more the desire to actually become a real estate professional grew. First I prayed about it, then I pumped my investment up again—the maximum this time—which I believe was twelve percent. Where I had started off with zero, one short year later, I had now acquired almost six thousand in stock funding and was eligible for a withdrawal as a first time home buyer. I was a little scared, but Cleveland had already told me that when I bought a building, I would make money every single month. He said that even when I closed on the building, I was going to walk away with a check.

I was dating another Keith at the time (geez, what was wrong with me?) The days that my mom and Keith 2 walked into the building with me, both had severely negative responses. They tried to discourage me in every possible way. Keith 2 visited the place before I purchased it and said, "What a foolish thing you're doing. Saving all of your money . . . can't even get your hair done. All for a building. How stupid is that?" Now mind you, he worked a job at a health center which seemed to be all he aspired to do in life at the time. Limited thinking! No wonder he couldn't be happy for me.

Now I can understand my mom, who saw the building after I purchased it, because she was born and raised believing that there were limitations on her life. That she, as a woman, was supposed to sacrifice everything for her husband and children without ever thinking of herself and what she wanted. But for me, somehow, some way, it was always a reality.

Their reactions would be my first lesson in keeping myself focused and surrounding myself with positive people in my life; ones who could help me hold the vision instead of tearing it down. Ladies let me tell you, being with a man who cannot be happy for you and progress with you is like taking heavy doses of poison. Injecting their negativity into your ears, your plans, your actions can weigh heavily on your heart. The jealousy and enviousness they can carry inside as they vacillate between loving you and hating you is a deadly weapon. And it doesn't stem from the fact that you're not giving them attention, love or great sex; it's all because you're courageous enough to follow your dream. I pressed through my mother's doubts, and Keith 2's bitterness, and became the property manager of my first building.

In February 1994, I made a down payment with funds I had saved and purchased my first building at the age of twenty-three. Cleveland was right. I actually came back with a check for nearly three thousand after closing. I was amazed! I moved in on the first floor, had a husband and wife as tenants upstairs and there was a small apartment downstairs that I intended to rent out to a college student.

With the help of Shelia Barber (Greg's wife), I learned how to repair my credit score rating. I contacted all of the companies, explained that I made immature decisions in the past, asked for restoration, disputed items on the accounts, and made significant improvements to my credit score. Initially I thought there was no escaping bad credit, boy was I wrong. Most companies really want to work out things with you to help restore your credit. You must make the first attempts of pushing through the fears, calling and sending letters to both the companies and all three credit bureaus requesting that items be removed from the credit history. It is okay to ask the company to help you restore your credit by removing some late fees. Also, settling a portion of the debt can give you the negotiating power to have late pays removed.

My dad, "Mr. Entroproknow" himself had encouraging words for me. "Nicko," (his nickname for me) when are you going to get building number two? I'm proud of you, girl." Those two sentences spoke life back into my mission. And it was a wonderful feeling that someone from my immediate family felt that I was truly making great decisions to benefit my life. When was I going to get building number two? Indeed!

Now the dynamics of my life had changed. I had paid off most of my debt, was not only collecting a rent check but was making a profit. The easy yet foolish choice would be to do my favorite thing—go on a spending rampage. But instead, I had been bitten by the real estate bug. The first thought that came to mind was—how about reinvesting and buy another building? And that's exactly what I did.

As I continued to make investment after investment, growing my business substantially, I was becoming the entrepreneur my dad said I could be. I was exceeding, not just meeting, all expectations I held for my professional life. Before I could blink twice, I had fifteen properties and was now the second vice president over the corporate division services at TNT. During what should have been the happiest time of my life, I had one major problem—the wrong man by my side. Everything in my life was going great except for the pains I experienced from being involved with a man who didn't honor me or himself. The more successful I became, the more hateful he became.

Though I heard about it in books, saw it in movies and on television, this would be the first time I personally experienced domestic violence in any form. It seems I couldn't do anything right. Everything was my fault. He resented my desire for more, and it became the strongest sentiment in that relationship for seven *long* years. I endured verbal, mental and, on occasion, physical abuse—all for the sake of what I thought was love once again. Inwardly, I knew differently. Even with everything I had going for me, I couldn't see a way out. My self-esteem had hit an all-time low, and the courage and qualities I valued in my business life—my career, taking risks, investing, helping my employees reach levels in their life they never thought was obtainable—were simply non-existent when it came to this man.

My employees rose above being Client Service Associates and Representatives to receiving titles like Officer, 2nd Vice President, Manager, etc., simply because I showed them that I believed in them. This was my survival technique as I walked through life, traveled through dark times alone, held my head up and kept up appearances. Where was my light? Where was that inner strength that could help me say, "To hell with him. I deserve better. God didn't make me or mold me to become someone else's punching bag, someone else's place to dump all their anger and frustrations."

The women who worked under me excelled and made it into positions they only dreamed about. Their successes became my light, and it pointed to the fact that they, too, derived strength—not just from what the opportunities I provided—but from the Source, the Creator! One morning I woke up, looked to my right and said, "What the hell is wrong with me? Why am I laying side by side with someone who has no respect for women, let alone me?" My whole life was dedicated to helping women get to the next level. I worked in a shelter, seeing abused women week in and week out, volunteered my time to encourage them, sympathized with them. The part that really kills is that I didn't even realize I, "Ms. Has it All Together," was one of them.

Somehow the illusion of my success was a better shield than any other. My businesses were going so well and no one could see through the role I portrayed, which enabled me to keep deeply hidden secrets of pain, hurt, degradation and mistreatment. Sometimes one simple thing could help lift my spirits. When I bought a new pair of shoes—a tall pair of gorgeous heels, sharp stilettos, or some funky mules—when I put them on my feet I felt empowered, even if it was only temporary. My thoughts were that when the world looks up to you, you have to put in an appearance; you have to "show up." Even when you know you're living a lie.

Now herein lies the lesson. Remember I had an issue with the young lady at the gym? The fact that she would teach one thing, but her habits, appearance and actions were the direct opposite? Life helped drive the point home. I was teaching women from self-esteem building to women from difficult circumstances, but I should have been in the class myself. I knew what to do; I just didn't do it. Those who can't do teach, right? My thinking held me a willing prisoner: I can't be that woman that travels from man to man. I'd soon become some worn out pair of shoes. So instead, I stayed and became just like that pair of shoes we tend to wear down to the ground then toss in the back of the closet. Women have a tendency to stay with men that are not good for them, just to make a point that is practically pointless. A man cannot love you when he doesn't love himself, yet you go on a mission to find a microscopic tidbit of love inside of him. This is God's job ladies, not yours. Spend your time more wisely, "praying for guidance" and then "acting upon God's plan for your life."

The day I decided to do just what the Snoop Dogg song states and *drop him like he was hot,* was the day I became empowered again. Right then and there, I vowed never to make that mistake again. Although I lived it, knew better and wanted better for myself, learning lessons on a personal level was a lot harder than getting out of that college debt. What is even more hilarious is that Keith 2 actually began to do something outside of his element a little later in life. You guessed it…real estate. He learned something from the Queen at least. Unfortunately for me, at age of twenty-seven, when I was ahead on my financial balance sheet, I was now hitting the ground at a negative two when it came to men.

Chapter 3: Questions to Ask Yourself

Entrepreneurship isn't easy, but nothing in life is…however, it is possible: what sacrifices will you make to achieve your entrepreneurial mission in life?

Who do you need to remove from your life that is, simply put, "a dream thief?"

Write in thoughts in your journal.

Corinthians 2:9— But as it is written: "Eye has not seen, nor ear heard, nor have entered into the heart of man the things which God has prepared for those who love Him."

"Let us rise up and be thankful, for if we didn't learn a lot today, at least we learned a little, and if we didn't learn a little, at least we didn't get sick, and if we got sick, at least we didn't die; so, let us all be thankful."

---Prince Gautama Siddharta

CHAPTER 4
MULES

A couple of months prior to making the final decision to leave Keith 2, one of the most tragic situations occurred in my life to date. This situation would help put many things into perspective for me. I can remember the day so very clearly— when once again, I was upset about my decision to even be in this relationship with a man who did not honor me.

After a long strenuous day at TNT and completing a few hours of community service, I headed for home. I was only blocks away from my house when I had a sudden urge to go to my parent's home. For some reason I just wanted to take some time and speak to my dad who, by now, was my best friend and a man that I began to hug as often as I could. So I quickly made a right turn off South Shore Drive and headed to my parent's home. It seemed like he was sitting there on the porch waiting just for me, when in actuality this was his "spot" since he retired and had nothing on his agenda but fishing. I know he loved my visits. And I loved being there with him just as much.

Not even ten minutes after I arrived, a Ford Explorer pulled up. The face on the driver's side seemed unfamiliar, but the woman on the passenger side was none other than my lovely sister, Netty. I couldn't believe how beautiful she looked on this day. Let me just share a brief story with you. Netty suffered from severe self-esteem issues. She had the most beautiful face and could sing like a hummingbird. Sadly though, unlike me whose weaknesses were men and shoes, Netty's weakness was food.

Netty had lived ten years in a place within the Chicago Housing Authority, more commonly known as "the Projects." One day my mom and I went to pick her up. My mom cried so hard because of what we saw—the apartment in total disarray, in nearly deplorable conditions. Netty stayed in my mother's home for ten years after that day. We sat in the kitchen once, and she was telling me how she wanted to get a job and have her own place. Something inside of her feared change so much that she didn't believe in herself at all.

Typically when I would see her, she was dressed in clothing better suited for a woman who didn't come from a family who cared. However, on this day that I sat on the porch with my father, she was gleaming and had on a beautiful peach dress with her hair pulled up and make-up done beautifully. A few weeks earlier she began to practice uplifting, self-motivation techniques; ones we would rehearse in the kitchen together. The many positive things I saw in her, she was finally beginning to see in herself. She spoke life back into her body, her mind and into her soul.

Netty had been living on her own now for three months. She got a job as an inventory clerk at a grocery store. It was a start, a place to move up from where she had become comfortable, and that was a huge step. She didn't move far from my parents because she still needed support. She courageously made a decision to change her life after twenty years of suffering and was now experiencing happiness beyond her imagination.

Oh, it was my great pleasure to see her walking up to the porch that day. I kept complimenting her, "Oh, Netty, you look so beautiful." She kept saying, "Huh?" So I repeated it again. And at her constant reply of, "Huh?" I ended up saying it over seven times. And finally she replied with a simple, "Thank you." I slipped her some pocket change and hours later I proudly watched her ride away.

The next morning I was working at TNT and my supervisor came into the meeting and said, "I need to speak with you right away." I was a complete workaholic and hated interruptions, but the look on my manager's face made me concerned. We stepped into the hallway and she said, "Your mother and father need you to call them at home." Naturally, my heart was pounding as I continued to probe and ask questions, but she kept simply saying, "You should call home."

I called the house and my dad answered, saying, "Nicky, Netty's in the hospital. You should come on home to meet us there." I was thinking, "Dad, what's wrong? Is it her varicose veins?" She had been back and forth to the hospital dealing

with the painful effects of varicose veins. No big deal. My
Dad told me to hurry home. I left work right then and there.
People kept asking to drive me home, but I refused their offers.
Thinking that nothing could be seriously wrong, I got in my
convertible, dropped the top and turned on the radio before a
sudden urge made me call home again.

This time my dad's voice was not so calm. In fact, he
seemed a little hysterical, which was completely out of character
for him. By this time I pleaded with my dad to tell me what
was wrong. "Netty is gone. Netty is gone." My father had
only cried once that I could remember—but hearing his sorrow
over the phone brought an instant sickness inside of me.

I made a U-turn and after that I really can't tell you all of
what happened next. I can only remember someone from my
job driving me to my parent's home. I was in the back seat
feeling as though everything, every movement was part of a
dream—someone else's dream. My dad helped me from the
car, holding me tight as he cried so hard. All I could manage to
ask was, "Where is she? Where is she?"

My co-worker graciously drove both of us to Little
Company of Mary Hospital. My mom and the rest of my family
were already there. I walked into the morgue, and against my
mother's wishes, wanted to see Netty. How could I believe
she was gone unless I saw it with my own eyes? I had just
witnessed her transformation the day before. She was
overweight and had been for many years, but yesterday she
looked better than ever. The happiest I'd ever seen her since
we were kids.

Every step I took into the morgue felt like my feet were weighed down as the long hallway seemed to grow before me. Minutes seemed like forever before I walked into the room and over to the cold, steel table where her body lay. I understood immediately why my mother didn't want me to see her. Netty had suffered a massive heart attack and rigor mortis had set in. Her hands and arms were frozen in a position behind her head. Her face was twisted in pain and it was a sight that left me filled with fear, misery and gave me nightmares for several weeks after her death.

At that moment I was so angry with God. "Why would you do this to her? How could you let this happen to her?" She spent most of her life being depressed, feeling down and never following her dreams. Finally, when she decided to take a stand in her life to change it, what she got back in return was death. What sense did that make? The thought itself brought an overwhelming sense of grief and unfairness.

Months afterward, as my anger dissipated, the fear went away and the nightmares subsided. Clearly God made sure I learned a lesson by speaking once again in that still voice saying, "Don't take life for granted. Your life belongs to me." And from Netty's transition I simply understood that it could end at any time. This motivated me to walk away from that painful relationship with Keith 2. I later learned that Keith 2 was just another young man traveling through life without a road map. I don't believe that his true intentions were to incite pain in my life. I simply believe in the old saying, "hurt people...hurt people." However, it is important to state that anyone who is not honoring you is completely unacceptable this is non-negotiable.

The experience with Netty also encouraged me to begin to truly live. Even though I began to make money—I didn't do much else for myself. I was still skeptical about spending money (except on shoes!) because I knew what it was like not to have any.

I started taking vacations, having overall pamper days and I even implemented a yearly "birthday celebration" for each member of my immediate family. I embraced life, cherished it. And although I missed my dear Netty, I learned something valuable from her death as I did from her life. When she decided to change, she did—and did it wholeheartedly—we could all see the effects that her inner change made on her outer appearance.

More than anything I will continue to hold that image of her walking up the porch draped in that peach dress, her dark brown eyes alive with power and confidence.

Chapter 4: Advice Summary

You've waited long enough…now let's get to work together. Time waits for no one. Put your written words into action. Begin today investigating everything you need to know about your chosen entrepreneurial industry. Make phone calls, blog, pull up information on websites, set-up interviews with like-minded people. Study your industry daily.

Let's get busy….LIVING.

Hebrews 6:11-12—And we desire that each one of you show the same diligence to the full assurance of hope until the end, that you do not become sluggish, but imitate those who through faith and patience inherit the promises

"Believe nothing, no matter where you read it, or who said it..unless it agrees with your own reason and your own common sense."   ---Prince Gautama Siddharta

Chapter 5

Combat Boots

Fighting to make your way

Like putting on a new pair of shoes, dropping that dead weight made me feel revived and ready to conquer the world. My career was still on the rise and now I could focus on another part of my dream. I was drawn back to the time when I was a child, when everything revolved around the community and our church. I truly understood that giving back and community work was just as important as excelling in my career. So just as I made it a habit to tithe ten percent of my income, I began to dedicate thirty percent of my time every week to giving back. I had already started spending time in shelters helping women build their self-esteem while I was working to build my own. I had accumulated many properties, was promoted to second vice president at TNT and was now making a major difference in the communities I was born and raised in as well as others just like it.

Although I spent many years working in corporate America, it was another burning desire of mine to leave my job and build my own successful career. I didn't have a clue of exactly what I wanted to do, but I knew that I had a lot of money and, by now, excellent credit. Stepping out on faith to do something courageous was another brick in the foundation. Several community events I attended with residents, politicians and other business owners were filled with constant complaints that steady, viable and sustainable businesses didn't exist in our communities. After a short time had passed, my thoughts ran to being part of the solution instead of complaining about the problem. Yes, it's a cliché, but it fit the situation. I once attended a community affair and a Chicago politician stood up strong and said, "I hear your complaints about what we don't have and understand it, but we must focus on determining how we can build a better quality of life for all." And then he delivered a powerful blow by saying, "With all of your love and desire to build a community, why not consider building a business? The same type of business that you're requesting "outside" people to come in to build. Build it yourself!"

Sleep didn't come easy that night. His words kept going through my mind over and over again. What kind of business could I build to help supply a need in my neighborhood? I prayed about this daily until I would receive an answer. Another business challenge? Of course, but then life doesn't just send a challenge on one front without testing another. This leads into the blast from my past.

Things were going so well. I had a house built from the ground up, rental property, two cars. I had everything on the surface that the average American person wants—everything except love.

What exactly is love? Looking back, I don't think I knew exactly what it was. Love means different things to different people. Women especially define love in terms of "I love you unconditionally," or it might be, "I love you as long as you do a, b and c." While men would put it terms that are drastically different—"I love you, in my own way." This may not translate into that unconditional, all-consuming, self-sacrificing kind of love that is expected on a deeper level. Few people can attain this kind of love because they, like me, have not learned one valuable lesson: love yourself first and foremost, then love others. Those who have not learned this important lesson are destined to repeat past mistakes.

I ran into a gentlemen from my past. He was educated, charming, hard-working, tall, dark and ab-so-lute-ly handsome. What's more is the man was ringing the doorbell to my brand new home. He too, had purchased a home built from the ground up in the very same neighborhood. By this time, I had been on several local television programs educating people on how to invest in bricks and mortar, and also how to work to build personal wealth. With that on his mind, he stood in my threshold, and in his own charming way, said, "Nicky, I saw you on television. I want you to teach me what it is you're doing in real estate. I want to become an investor, too." Music to my ears as well as those belonging to many other women. Sometimes men have a problem learning things from a woman—especially when it comes to money.

We would begin our little journey by doing what I love to do anyway: finding the right investment properties and turning them into a plus on the financial balance sheet.

So the fun began. By this time I was a pro. I could walk into a completely dark building with stilettos on, jumping over debris and mice without breaking a sweat. However, Mr. Jones wasn't anywhere close to being ready for some of the experiences he would encounter. Though I was a serious person, some people knew me to be a prankster. On the third building we walked into, I decided it was time to do something to get Mr. Jones to lighten up. When most people entertain the idea of opening a new business or embarking on a new venture, there is fear of the unknown, skepticism and resistance to change. Every building I walked him into looked like a bad investment to him. So I waited until we went into the darkest, creepiest property. I took a few steps in to check out the scene first and noticed that he was a little shaky just walking behind me. This should have been a sign right then and there. I strolled through the building, not knowing if crackheads or anyone else were already on the property. I didn't look back at Mr. Jones as I said, "You know, I've walked into properties and found animals and all kinds of things…" Now that's one thing I *wasn't* joking about. I had visited over two hundred properties at this point and could write a book about those experiences alone. "You never know what you're going to find in these properties, Mr. Jones, so be prepared."

Now I'm walking tall, strong and sexy in my beautiful new pumps, going from the living room to the dining room as though nothing was amiss. Suddenly I turned and screamed, "Get out!

Somebody's in here!" Mr. Jones darted for that door so fast—he didn't even check to see if I got out with him. I laughed my heart out! Once he realized there was nothing to be frightened about, all he could do was laugh, too. Mission accomplished—he lightened up.

After that incident, he began to see the buildings in a different light. Instead of uncertainty, he now saw the potential of what could be done with them. His visions became more clear and precise about what a good investment was and which buildings didn't pass muster. Everything that looks dilapidated, grungy or unsophisticated is not always the way it appears. Trusting your judgment and having a good sense of what you're working toward is key to being successful. It helps strip away the surface and allows you to see the real value. Now that Mr. Jones and I were on the same page, we could certainly change the dynamics of our lives on a financial level. Somehow this also spilled over to a personal level as well.

One year from the time he rang my doorbell, Mr. Jones asked me to marry him. I graciously accepted, all while knowing that he had a past history with women that didn't speak to having a successful relationship. However, like so many women, I believed I could change him. I saw something in him that was different. There was something about me that would *make* him different.

Now all the signs were there—three children with three different mothers, old girlfriends showing up before the wedding—and that was the tip of the iceberg. I became a wife, a business owner, and a stepmother to the two children who would stay with us periodically. We sold my house and I moved into his while we waited to purchase the one we would stay in and build as a family. A woman came to his door to "get her shoes." A pair of brown, scrawny, tore-up from the floor-up, missed their chance to be in the garbage—shoes. She came nevertheless, actually trying to get a little face time with my soon-to-be husband. The pain-stricken expression on her face when she saw me was one thing I will never forget. Somehow, it's easy for our minds to be deceived. I kept thinking, her loss was my gain. Hadn't I made that same mistake before? That night when Jackie had shown up to speak with Keith, and I thought I had won a prize because he chose me over her. Somehow I hadn't learned my lesson.

So, the caution signs went off—not the red light, not the green light, but the yellow one that insists you pause a long while before going forward. I interpreted it my own way and took that "C" in caution and turned it into CHANGE. I figured that I had an educated brother with a very good job, his own things, his own home and who learned from me how to build a real estate empire. If he could change from being mediocre in the finance department, then he could definitely change his appetite for other women.

We started off right. We went to marriage counseling for sixteen weeks, wrote out the goals for our lives, for our family and our future. Through every phase I was beginning to believe that caution sign was a fluke. Well, I would soon learn that when God gives you insight, heeding that wisdom is the best option. We're constantly living in a world that doesn't even exist—the fantasy world within our own minds—and what we actually want or desire can overshadow the wisdom from God that says, "It's not for you." A friend of mine, Naleighna Kai, once told me: sometimes the answer to our prayers is a "No or not right now," and we don't want to hear that. She also said that sometimes on one level we pray for peace and harmony; then because we're lonely (or horny) we accept someone in our lives that will bring in the exact opposite. Praying for one thing, accepting another. The signs are always there. Sometimes we choose not to listen. I was no different than a lot of other people.

Less than a year into the marriage, issue after issue prevailed. The main challenge was one he experienced all of his life . . . *women*. This time, I had to step up and take full responsibility. I went into reactive mode right away. My relationship with God became first and foremost, and I did what it took to strengthen that connection first. Then I began to study and learn the dynamics around the makings of a successful marriage. Everything that I thought it took to be a great wife and stepmother, I dove right in. I became a phenomenal cook, a sex expert and spent numerous hours finding ways to become even closer to the three stepchildren who brought me joy. The fact of the matter was real simple, I could change every single thing about me, but I most certainly could not change another person. Believing that you have the power to change someone else will always lead to failure.

Now that my mind was open and I realized assessing the situation and the players (no pun intended) was important, I had to re-evaluate myself. Why did I constantly choose men who were not right for me? What was I missing? This assessment period forced me to search the root cause of my actions, which took me back to the Mary Jane days. I had to admit that even though the imagery on the outside looked like I was at the top of my game, I was still suffering from low self-esteem . . . just like my sister Netty. On the inside I never believed that I deserved to be with a good, respectable, successful man.

During this self-assessment period instead of pointing the fingers at my husband or Keith 1 and 2, the fingers pointed directly to me, and me alone. My choices, my actions, my life. It wasn't that these three individuals didn't show me who they were from the beginning, it was that I chose to overlook the obvious signs. I had a God complex, assuming that I—an attractive, hard-working, determined woman who would look good on any man's arms——had the power to change someone other than myself. I had the magic wand with the ability of making a man from mediocre to king of the castle. Wrong! Now I had to go to the back of my closet, pull out those combat boots, slip them on, tie them up and get to stepping. The real work was just starting.

There is a major difference from the love you receive from God versus the love that you can receive from man. God's love is eternal, where man's love can be fleeting. People love you until something goes wrong, then they disregard you or have an overwhelming, consuming hate for you. True love sees beyond your faults. True love forgives. True love understands that people make mistakes.

One of the most difficult things in life is to review your own faults. It takes courage to stand before that mirror and say, "Stop blaming everybody. You are part of this problem."

One of the next things on the agenda was to understand why I desired this need for love so badly. Not that it's a bad thing to want love, but to feel as if you need it from another human being instead of first accepting the love from God who is the source of our supply, then loving yourself next. This is the basis for a countless number of issues. Once I narrowed it down, my personal, emotional and spiritual things to do list held two items: time for me to learn to love myself and how to depend on the Lord instead of a man. I will be the first to admit that this journey is not easy, but I kept feeling that breakthrough moment as I started each day with prayer.

Another breakthrough came by removing every negative entity in my life, but the main breakthrough was accepting that my husband had this long-term issue. Instead of judging him, I prayed for him; but in actuality, I spent the majority of the time praying for myself. It was time to be a little selfish and, for the record, that's okay—because we, as women, give so much to others in our lives we don't take time for ourselves. The truth of the matter is that as the center in a household or in intimate relationships if we fall apart, everything else follows suit. So sometimes sticking with a plan of self first then helping others means we gain our center, and then we have something to share with others.

The moment my daily ritual of prayer became second nature, it led me to the realization that I had even more dreams which hadn't been realized. At this point, I decided to go back to the dream of building a business within the community. One cold winter morning in our beautiful grey stone, I woke up about three o'clock screaming in my sleep, because I finally knew what I wanted to do. Since my childhood, I had been in awe while looking in the windows of shoe stores, always fantasizing about those beautiful shoes being on my feet. Every time I felt down or the lack of love from men in my life, buying a new pair of shoes always made me feel temporarily empowered. Shoes had a way of making me happy, and I knew that other women shared this same passion.

When I woke from that dream, the message from God was very clear. Now it was up to me. I could allow this dream to die right away, which is typical of people with great ideas, or I could choose to give it life. Now the truth of the matter was that I had never worked in a retail store environment before, but that little fact wasn't going stop me. One thing had always been clear to me, if you don't know something, you always have an opportunity to learn it. So it was time to get on the learning train again, and it's not like I hadn't been on the express to the banking industry, the local to stocks and investing, and finished up with a commuter ride into the real estate world. All aboard!

The very next morning, I made thirty signs which read:

I want to buy your building, please call me. Followed by my number.

I drove down Cottage Grove Avenue, which was filled with distressed properties—a far cry from a place where one would open a store that was supposed to rival the kind on Rodeo Drive. The community, called Bronzeville, was once filled with successful businesses. During the recession in the 1950's, a lot of those businesses closed creating a void that no one knew how to fill. Black people were living in the high point of prime property just a few blocks from the lakefront, minutes from downtown and with connections to every major expressway in Chicago. One would say my choice to build a business in this area is the first major mistake in retail; typically it is. On the other *foot*, this vision to build the property somewhere in this area was a burning desire in my heart. My logic for even entertaining the thought of having a business in the community was simple: the city was beginning to reinvest in the area, pumping millions of dollars into redevelopment with the intent to usher in another group of people and culture that are vastly different from the brown-skinned, enterprising people who had been there for years.

Driving past the places many investors had overlooked, the risk-taker in me stood at army attention. I already knew it would be hard work to market and promote the type of business I had in mind, but I never shied away from a challenge. If I put my time, money and energy into this business idea, it could—and would—prosper. No matter the area, no matter that people thought my idea of a shoe salon flanked by a car-filled lot on one side and a vacant lot on the other within the heart of Bronzeville was totally insane. Yet, I remained optimistic.

As I traveled that morning placing signs on every building I came across, there was one in particular that stood out the most. The windows were covered so I couldn't see inside, but measuring it from the outside, it was a lot of space. In my mind's eye I would build a business rivaling that of ones on the Magnificent Mile, one that could hold enough women to host community events right in my place of business instead of running from shelter to shelter.

I left a note and walked quietly to my car, praying all the way, knowing I wouldn't visit any more properties or leave any other notes that day. Now there was much more work to do: getting incorporated, devising a business plan, securing financing, building a website and, the biggest hurdle yet, getting the community to buy into this idea. Actually the community would buy into any possible retail idea to help get something going and the alderman was a vision-forward woman who did everything by the book. I met with her to discuss my plans first.

I could never understand businesses that would build in communities and never give back. I saw it from every place that I lived, but especially in the African American community. Other cultures would come in, conduct business and never attend a community meeting, or have a day to give back to the people who patronize them daily. Sometimes they treated the people who placed money in their pocket without any respect, simply because their options seemed limited. Those are pimps —just without the suit, that big old hat and the tricked out Cadillac. I couldn't run a business in any community and not contribute to it. Community residents should hold business owners accountable for giving back to the community which is serving them.

Residents in some deprived neighborhoods constantly settle for less. Recently, I went to a local gas station which is located in a predominately African-American area and witnessed the most repulsive client service I could ever imagine. The cashier, possibly the owner, had received his money from a young gentlemen, but was more concerned with collecting the money from other customers waiting in the line than finishing the young man's transaction. Without any hesitation the young gentlemen asked nicely, "Can you please turn my pump on sir?" To my surprise the clerk screamed back, "Wait a minute!" Then he said out loud, "He's acting like a damn animal." I couldn't believe my ears. How could he disrespect this man who had just supported his business? I stepped in immediately and said to him in a voice loud enough for everyone to hear, "You have the nerve to disrespect him? Your words were unkind and completely unnecessary." I told him that I was disappointed in his behavior and chose to take my money somewhere else. Everyone else in line heard what he had said to this young man, yet everyone remained in line. Please note that in this neighborhood, many residents have complained continuously about being mistreated at this gas station, yet they still support it. Why?

Early on I set a goal that I wouldn't let a single day go by without doing something relating to my new business plan, even if just made a phone call. I set up a meeting with my Alderman, Toni Preckwinkle, and community liaisons to discuss my plans. They loved the idea and supported it wholeheartedly. Within one week, mostly all of the legal aspects of starting the business were done. All was going well. The second week, reality set in. I didn't know *anything* about running a retail store. I needed direction on the first steps. How do I buy? Where do I get my products? How much do I buy? Where do I get a register from? How do I pay sales taxes? I didn't have a clue; but I knew who did!

I had developed a list for my personal development, spiritual development and real estate endeavors, so I needed to put one together for this retail business. I reviewed websites and did a little library research to make a list of other successful shoe businesses, and then I called them one by one to ask their expert opinion on how I could execute this retail store. Seventy percent of the people I called wouldn't speak to me. I couldn't believe how people felt intimidated by others. My major issue in life was how I felt about myself and about my choices in men. On a business level, I always wanted to share and see people achieve success.

The journey into the retail side of business was tougher than I ever imagined. I can't tell you how many people shut the door in my face or said things to discourage me. I knew that I would need to press on and, thanks to the thirty percent that would talk to me, I would make it. One wonderful woman, who owned Gabrielle's on the north side of Chicago, opened up her heart, her mind and her store for me to learn. I also had someone else to invite me into their store but later learned it was for all the wrong reasons. This individual only wanted to know my plans because they had every intention of blocking my path. This time when the caution sign blinked into view, I listened and kept my focus on the people who would help. Being treated so poorly by other entrepreneurs who had the same passions stopped hurting after a while. One major thing helped me in that process. I accepted that those people didn't understand that God knew their address and He would not get their blessings mixed with anyone else's. All I could do was pray for them. One thing more is that I knew I would never become one of them.

Each day as I began to understand my destiny more and more the fear dwindled and my focus stayed on the mission. Building a business on a desolate street is no easy task. I was tired of hearing complaints about what our community lacked. I would be a pioneer, the brave one, and provide what was needed. I loved everything about shoes ... loved the way they felt when being slipped on my feet. I loved the versatility that shoes added to my wardrobe.

Any woman can tell you it is an empowering experience when you find the right pair of shoes. However, I could not just open any old kind of shoe store ... no way ... no how. I had to open one that defined every essence of a woman. I began with the color first. I wanted to take women back to their childhood days and dazzle them with the color pink. Pink is a simple but bold color that can be sassy, sultry and a symbol of a woman's touch. Then the interior of the store had to be comfortable, relaxing, inviting. I wanted women to feel like queens when they walked in the door; royalty if they were going to grace my business with their glorious presence; valued because they could possibly spend money in my store which, in turn, would keep the doors open indefinitely.

The chairs I selected were massive, relaxed and an antique style. Glass tables to showcase the products would be adorned with beautiful pink stands and pink hat boxes. Details and attention were put into the café station so when people entered into the shoe salon they felt catered to. Since I was a bargain shopper myself, I knew that just because I didn't spend thousands at a time on purchases, didn't mean that I couldn't feel like I had every time I entered a store.

Most businesses have strayed away from great customer service because the Internet has become the way they handle things. They can conduct sales without ever seeing a face, hearing a voice or connecting with an individual. I love interacting with a woman who is on the hunt for a great pair of shoes. She walks in under the impression that she really knows what she is looking for. She is on a "shoe high," the same kind of high she would get when walking into a special event with a sharp dress, hair laid, make-up on point, while watching the eye of every man to ensure all eyes are on "The Queen." This is how a serious shoe shopper views a trip to the store. Yes, I say this with ease and experience … a simple pair of shoes can instantly change the way a woman feels.

Any information other entrepreneurs tried to hide from me, God somehow saw to it that I received everything I needed to start … and more. I signed up to attend that show and arrived on the first day ready to shop. Amazingly, that same lady who told me that the next show was *months* away was the first person I laid eyes on when I walked in. *Hmmmmmmmm.*

Understand this point clearly: if you are focused on your dream, and something is for you, no one can keep it away from you. No one! I can't say enough that God knows your address; information is in abundance to Him. Someone, somewhere taught you what you are doing. Why would you selfishly deny success to someone else? I walked up to her with a smile, gave her a hug and said, "have a great show." It always feels good to take the high road and show people great examples of being a lady . . . and a professional. I am quite certain that the woman will never forget that I wasn't snippy or sarcastic, and that her actions toward me showed me the true fabric of her soul.

Something inside of me was changing. My husband had refused to participate in this business even though we had envisioned running a family business together—the ladies and his buddies were a little more important. At first I was hurt over the situation since things did not seem to work in my favor; but here I was again, in a loveless relationship with only God lifting me up on all sides. I would be remiss if I didn't mention that I have wonderful, God-fearing girlfriends. There are two in particular, Janine and Tiffany, who held the vision strong even when others couldn't manage a single encouraging word. My "soul" sisters prayed with me, fasted and believed in the miracle of my life turning around.

My friends marveled at my vision of opening the store and they supported me until the ends of earth. I love them dearly for their commitment. There were some people close to me, however, who became extremely jealous and envious in ways that I had not previously experienced; I had not expected that, and it took me by surprise. When you are working to build your dreams, some people take it personally and because they lack the sense of direction, motivation and encouragement to do the same, they find fault in everything you do. It comes out in the smallest things, like little verbal hints, "Yeah, she has new friends around all of a sudden, now she doesn't have time for me," and things of that nature.

As an entrepreneur you'll spend more hours working than on an average nine-to-five job, but somehow everything about you bothers them because they can't accept that some things must change. In your mind you must say, "Yes, I'm evolving. I'm embarking upon a new life and in this new life some sacrifices must be made." The majority of the sacrifice is money and time. It's nothing personal. Family time and friend time is all the same; even "me" time goes by the wayside. Just like I did when saving money so my investments in stocks could increase, I started doing my hair and nails myself; any other luxury items (well, except shoes, of course) were forbidden. Still I did my best trying to juggle all of the events that landed on my calendar: from bridal showers, wedding and baby showers to birthday celebrations, special engagements, etc. The fact still remained that time management was crucial, especially in the first five to seven years of starting a business.

The people on your side must understand that things will be a little different, but only temporarily. Your true friends will be there during the storms as well as on the days where the sun shines brightly. Just like the Bible speaks of a tree that bears no good fruit, it goes without saying that in order for the tree to flourish, some of the branches need to be pruned; the rotten fruit plucked. This extracting or "pruning" process was good for me ending several long-term relationships with catty women who I found, through my current endeavors, had always secretly disliked me. As I released them with ease, comfort and joy, they were soon replaced with additional love from genuine friends and family. Just like those greedy business owners who shut the door directly on my pointed toe stilettos, friends turned foes could slide out of my life as easy as one could slip off a pair of mules. Once a woman, whose name escapes me, came to the shoe salon and spoke on the fact that people, like fruit, can ferment and become rotten if we hold onto them past their season. I was maturing, and it felt so good when I began repairing any side effects left from broken relationships in all forms.

April 28, 2005, was my deadline. I purchased the property at 4518 S. Cottage Grove as a condominium store front with an unfinished basement (then it was just a crawl space) and had it completely rehabbed in four months. Yes, there were some lingering tendrils of fear, absolutely; but I did it anyway. Fear could not stop what was fated by God. Disobedience and not following my heart could have put a halt to everything, but I had to learn a technique that will be with me until there isn't a single breath left to flow through my lungs—encourage myself.

It was only a few days before the salon was set to open, and you have to know that no one could have been happier than me. Every naysayer had criticized the location, told me the economy was too bad to start a business and every other negative thing that one could imagine. The eye that I kept on purchasing the right shoes to place on brand new glass shelves is the same one I kept on the prize.

The doorbell rang and I ran to the door, excited that I would be greeting my first new client. My new standard greeting, "Hi, welcome to Sensual Steps Shoe Salon. Are you looking for anything in particular?" flowed from my lips. The angry man looked at me, heated disgust filling his eyes, as he asked, "What is this place?" Taken aback, I managed to reply, "We are a women's shoe boutique." This man, who I had never seen before that moment, had the nerve to say, "Girl, why would you build this place on a block where there are no other businesses? You are bound to fail."

My heart froze. My mind stood still. The only thing that I could say was, "God will ensure my success." I wish I could scream to the world how detrimental negative words can be to someone. Even if you don't understand someone's vision or mission, even if you believe they are nuts for following their dreams, don't pour salt on them. Negative words are like poison in the minds of others. The more appropriate thing to say is, "Keep praying, and let God lead you." Tell them that you will be praying with them as well. Some don't know God's plans for their own lives, let alone someone else's. There aren't too many things that make me angry, but this one particular thing is like having a sliver of glass slipping around inside my shoes.

After I delivered my quick kill answer to this total stranger, I locked the door. I lowered my head, looked down at my feet, and I cried. Every ounce of courage and bravado, every ounce of faith slipped from my mind, from my heart and from my soul. "God, what am I doing? I've invested everything that I have into this place, and it is built on an abandoned block! Oh God, why have you forsaken me." I cried really hard for about five minutes. At the lowest points in life, something so strong inside, like a surge of electricity, will flow through the body forcing you to move.

After my crying spell, I felt a bolt hit me and I ran to the big, beautiful mirror in my store. I took a good look at myself and said, "He doesn't know who I am." My chin lifted as I followed with, "He doesn't know that this is God's plan for my life." That man, that *stranger*, had me twisted. I had put things in place to keep me going strong after the actions and words of friends and family who doubted my mission. How could I let him sway me? Once again I was reminded that self-esteem can be an ongoing battle. Situations may arise to test it, to bolster it and to make you reflect. Every positive affirmation that my mind could gather at that moment came out of my mouth, counteracting his negative words . . . his angry energy. I didn't even realize that I was speaking positive affirmations. People sometimes knowingly, and unknowingly, can speak death into something of yours that God is giving life. Remain prayerful; listen to God's conscious voice.

Moments later, I was back on my toes ready for the show down. It was WAR! He would not be the only one who felt this way. I would have to quickly wrap myself around the fact that everyone had an opinion that could be entirely different from mine, but it doesn't mean that I have to value or act upon their feelings. Sesvalah, the author of *Speak into Existence*, says that when negative people come to you that way, it's best to say a simple, "Thanks for sharing, but that's not what I believe." When people call on the phone ready to dump gossip or pour salt into your plans, get off the phone as quickly as possible. Just say, "Girl, I'm in the middle of something right now" or "I'll have to call you back." Sesvalah is so right! I will definitely respect people because they are entitled to their opinions, but I will not carry the weight of their negative words on my shoulders or in my soul.

The day of my grand opening, I placed a beautiful pink treasure chest near the front door so anyone could donate new and gently worn shoes for less fortunate women in shelters. Seven wonderful girlfriends and two staff members all anxiously waited on our new clients. Shoe cakes, martinis, fashion shows, a live band and, most importantly, all the lovely footwear that would provide an orgasmic shoe shopping experience. Everything was intact. We made over ten grand in a single day!

A week after my grand opening, Janine provided me with a book titled "The Dynamic Laws of Prosperity," by Catherine Ponder. She said, "Nicky, if you want your business to prosper, make God your business partner. Find out how by reading this book." Unfortunately, I was in the state of "busy-ness" and tossed this book to the side with many other uplifting books that I seemed to get as boring gifts all the time.

Little did I know that right at that moment, when I tossed the book on the shelf with the others, I was tossing away a key piece of my future.

Chapter 5: Questions to Ask Yourself

What will be the name of your company? Make sure the name is available and not being used often in other ways.

What colors will you use in your business, whether it is mobile, bricks and mortar, shared spaced, etc.? Colors enhance or decrease the shopping mood of your clients. Learn about the right colors for your business.

Some of your research is done. Let's build your Business Plan. Where do you want to open? Get the demographics, find out who your customers will be.

Don't stop there; more research must be done. Enroll with several female business organizations in your community. Become a member of the Urban League or a business entity that specializes in assisting small businesses in your area.

No, the work is not over yet. Contact your local politicians to request a meeting. Once your business plan is completed, you want to find a location sooner rather than later and may need the assistance of local leaders to obtain permits and things of that nature.

Ready, Set…WORK!

Philippians 3:13-14 Brethren, I do not count myself to have apprehended; but one thing I do, forgetting those things which are behind and reaching forward to those things which are ahead, I press toward the goal for the prize of the upward call of God in Christ Jesus.

"However many holy words you read, however many you speak, what good will they do you if you do not act on upon them?"

---Prince Gautama Siddharta

CHAPTER 6
PUMPS

Only a mere five years later, I was completely down on my luck again. My store was losing more money than I could count. People stopped shopping because of the "recession." At least that's what the world wanted to call it. Let's do the math. There are 97 million women (according to the U.S. Census) between the ages of 18 and 64, and for my purposes, they all (typically) have feet. People are making purchases every single day. I had to get out of a negative mindset so I could tap into the energy I needed to reach those people. When people start believing that there is a recession, negative thinking becomes a way out. It's the easy route to say that *everything in the world is going bad right now so it's okay that I'm in this situation.* That's like pronouncing that accepting failure is okay, so you might as well go ahead and lose everything.

There is something much bigger than the existence of this world. It's the Being that created it. What is His master plan for your life? He designed our lives to be filled with prosperity including great health, happiness, wealth and peace. I say peace because when living in a state of chaos, God's voice can't get through. You need that inner peace so you can enjoy the time you're slated to be on this earth. Naleighna constantly says that, "God did not put us here for the sole purpose of paying bills! Some people get so caught up in the day to day things that they forget there is a higher purpose for everyone's life. We are all lessons and blessings to each other."

Good health is another major point. Without good health, energy levels can become so low and can lead to the inability to motivate yourself to act or react. People primarily focus on health challenges instead of thinking about the great attributes they have to offer. In some cases that focus overcomes you to the degree that it can break you. Prior to reading self-help and inspirational books, I thought prosperity was just about finances. I was completely wrong. Having experienced health challenges myself, I learned from personal experience the impact it could have. I had plenty of money at the time but couldn't get out of bed, which meant I couldn't spend it or enjoy it. So traveling this road helped me to define what true prosperity meant— how to have a great balance in my life and to change defeatist or negative thinking and turn it into victory.

Now enters another phase of my life. The marriage was falling apart and my accounts were registering below zero balances. Overdraft fees alone were almost like paying another monthly mortgage. The credit cards were back up to the limit, and I couldn't keep a dime in my pocket. Business was slow and the remaining real estate investments faltered as tenants couldn't pay their rent. I could not believe it. Here it is, I thought that I was the most financially stable person and would remain that way for the rest of my life. Credit companies that would extend a line of credit for anything I required, were now taking things away. The banks that made thousands off my business and investments, refused to give me a bail-out program. Financial wealth and physical health were almost parallel to me, with money slipping through my fingers like grains of sand. My focus was now in tune with wondering what else could possibly go wrong. I had just about given up on myself. Janine, ever the positive one, said, "Nicky, snap out of this! God entrusted you with so much in the past, you have been so faithful in giving to others—and even now you haven't stopped tithing. God would not fail you now." Truthfully, Janine was getting on my last damn nerve (keep in mind that it's highly irregular for me to use foul language, but I cursed on this day). I just felt that with everything I had accomplished, God had deserted me.

Janine was in the passenger seat of my car and asked that I go home and pick up the entrepreneurial finance book for her, one that was written by Professor Steven Rogers. I pulled over in front of my home, darted inside, went to look for the book only to find it missing. My books are normally in one central place, so I couldn't understand why I couldn't find the book she asked for. I tore through the house looking every place I could think of. I knew that if I didn't find that book, she would get on my nerves until I did. Janine was an avid reader.

Out of over one hundred books on my shelf, I finally saw the one titled, *The Dynamic Laws of Prosperity.* I said, "Hmmmm, this sounds interesting. A little familiar, but interesting… I'm going to give her this book and shut her up."

The most peculiar thing happened as I skipped to the door. As soon as my shoe hovered over the threshold, I could hear a voice. God's voice never sounds to me the way it would if someone was talking right across from me. This particular voice was so loud and clear in my mind: "Nicole, *you* are going to read this book." I said, "No, no, no—oh no! I need some dinero, some cashola, some money from you, God. I'm not about to read this thick book. I don't have time. I need some *money*! " God said again, in that same loud voice, "You *will* read this book." The second time scared me a little. I then walked to the car, with a little less skip in my step, because now I had to break the news to Janine that I couldn't find the book she really wanted. Next I had to explain to her that God was demanding that I keep and read the book that I actually did find for her. Out of the many hundreds of books that I own, I don't know what made me grab that one. So I got in the car and told Janine what transpired and ended with my experience at the threshold.

Janine lightly snatched the book from my hand. She did not have her reading glasses with her, so she held the book very close to her face and began to peel through the pages. "Now Nicky, I gave you this book *four years ago!* I can't believe you haven't read a single sentence. There isn't even a pen mark in this book! I told you that if you wanted your business to prosper, that God has to be your business partner."

All I could do was apologize and commit to reading the book. I began that very day. This was the day when my life began to change for the better. I decided to go through a chapter per day. After one week of reading the book, I could feel my faith being restored; I could feel my vessel being refilled with precious oil.

The story in the Bible that warms my heart is a miracle story of the empty vessel. A woman whose husband had died, did not have anything—not even food for her children—only a pot of oil. She was commanded by Elisha to borrow empty vessels from her neighbors and then to pour the oil from the pot she had. As she poured, the oil miraculously kept coming and coming until every single pot was filled. She told Elijah what happened, and he instructed her to go sell the oil. She was to pay the man her husband owed, then use the rest to buy food for herself and her family.

This story matched my life in many ways. My vessel was empty and a single book of wisdom, along with the encouragement of a good friend, helped to fill all the empty vessels in my life: the vessels of faith, hope, love and prosperity.

So I called Janine again, screaming, (I always scream when I'm excited—and scare the heck out of everyone) and I said, "Janine there is help for us. You were right. I apologize for having been so doubtful."

Janine said, "It's okay. It wasn't your time then, but it is certainly your time now." I understand now, as I had not before, that the book and its powerful information would not have had as big of an impact on me until I hit this low point in my life. When one is down on their luck, like Job of the Bible had

experienced with the loss of his home, his wife, his children—
there is no place to go but up. Sometimes it takes a book, a
word or a person. For me it was a person who introduced me
to a book that had the information that was needed (four years
before I needed it), then for God to say, "Listen up, woman!"

So I'm saying to you, the person reading this book, "Listen
up." Open your mind because you will not believe the next set
of events that transpired.

Somehow I would have to convince Janine to step
completely out of her comfort zone. We have a great deal in
common ... Janine is a shoe fanatic at well! Even though I'm
mentioning her in the Pump chapter, Janine is a straight-up
stiletto woman. Now let me also tell you that she is one of the
most humble, loving, compassionate, spiritual, trustworthy and
peaceful women I have ever met in my life. She is a walking
book filled with so much knowledge, but *she did not like to
speak publicly.*

Ironically, we both paid for a speech coaching class but
didn't take the time to attend. We both knew that it was in
Divine Order for us to do a lot more speaking engagements; I
would put Janine on the spot quite often at community events.
This should have served as a heads-up for her. One day I called
her knowing she wasn't going to like what I had to say. "You
must start conference calls next week! There are women out
there hurting. They need to understand the power that God
gave them and need someone trustworthy like you to help them."
There was silence on the other end of the line, so I continued
with, "As much as I love you, I can't just have your wisdom all
to myself any longer."

When Janine would speak on spiritual things, she had a way of making people feel like they were the only ones who mattered in the world at that moment. She supported me through financial difficulties, marital issues and many other things that I won't mention at this time. There are so many things that I learned from these experiences, one of which is that spiritual and personal development is an ongoing process. It is not something accomplished in just one sweep of a year, two years—or even a decade. As we grow physically and, just as changes occur that we can see in the mirror, so does our inner being—the spirit that animates our bodies. So it goes without saying that every challenge, every milestone, every experience is all designed to help us reach the next level of spiritual development. We take the lessons learned along with us to help get through the next level and to gain wisdom along the path.

Let's just say that Janine, with a little resistance, agreed to the conference call idea. I called our backbone right away— my girlfriend, Tiffany. Janine is courageous, a risk-taker, positive and very vocal in personal settings. Tiffany, on the other hand, is more calm, humorous and feisty. What they have in common, however, is their spiritual foundation. Tiffany is a classic pump woman, but like Janine, won't go too far out of her element. Tiffany is like the outside of an Oreo cookie, and Janine is the center. I, on the other hand, am more of an Almond Windmill cookie. Either way, just like your favorite cookie, women can be sweet, different, a mouthful and something to look forward to. People often tell me when they meet my two closest friends, that I am blessed for having such good people around me.

Remember the old saying, *it takes one to know one?* My reply is that you must first **be** a good friend to **have** a good friend. My friends and I were beginning another journey that would lead to many wonderful opportunities . . . more than words can describe.

First, I contacted women who I knew were hurting financially, mentally or spiritually—it didn't matter which. I called every woman I could and told them about our new conference calls, and that they were free of charge. Janine ordered the books we would use on a wholesale basis and we began a spiritual movement that has helped change the lives of every woman involved. In short, women that had been about to lose their homes were suddenly no longer in foreclosure. Women who lost their jobs became employed. Women who were mentally broken had found stability and strength.

Collectively, we pulled together, prayed together and learned together. They only had to purchase the books necessary to follow along with the conference. There's a big reason we could take the time and do this without charging a dime. I read something recently that speaks to this point. Louise L. Hay, in her book, *Empowering Women*, states that if you focus on doing the thing you love, the money will follow.

Everyone built a "vision board" for their lives. Mine read the following and behind each request was a strong affirmation that I read every single day:

1) faith and favor restoration;
2) lifelong prosperity, no more temporary financial gain;
3) happiness, health and true love;

4) Sensual Steps, Inc.—to have an innumerable company of angels to work there and clients to shop;

5) to sell my home.

Number six was kind of farfetched, but I do realize now that there is no request made of the Creator that is not without His ability to manifest:

6) to be on a reality show on a major television network station that played into the homes of at least 10 million viewers.

Would you believe because of number one on my vision board, faith and favor restoration, that in the words of Naleighna Kai, "doors of opportunity were opening faster than I could walk through them."

Tiffany, Janine and I began a journey that is changing our lives and the lives of others. We still conduct morning conference calls on a daily basis, inviting women on a mission for change and praying, then working, until something happens.

With this in mind, I applied for a reality television show by sending a video application. Would you believe that a network television station called me back! I even flew to Los Angeles for five days of airing. Then I made it to another stage in the application process so they came to the comfort of my home to film the store and a private shoe soiree. The taping was amazing. Every day I kept waking up wondering if I was dreaming or not. However, God would pinch me on the shoulder and say, "Yes, you are living this dream…it is real."

Not only was everything on my vision board coming to fruition, but the number of callers on our conference line grew immensely; even men began to join us. I've witnessed miracle after miracle simply because people dared to do something different. It's a simple notion that reading a book, praying, trusting, believing that God's word is true, could enhance every aspect of life. Notice that the first focus was on the spiritual development, and everything else was a given. The focus wasn't on money or finding a way out of all the issues that almost knocked me off my feet, it was all about my connection to God and strengthening that connection through the things that can easily happen every day: prayer, affirmation, reading a book, aligning myself with those who could hold my vision.

After making it to the final stages of being on a large network station, the only thing that came to mind was, "How could God do something so big for little old me?" I kept believing that these dreams were too big and they belonged to someone else. I saw everyone else as a giant and saw myself in miniscule terms. But let me tell you this, God makes no distinction between the two. It's the main reason that David was able to slay Goliath—he found favor with God and recognized God first and foremost. Size had nothing to do with it—faith and action, hand in hand, helped to slay the giant in David's life—and moved mountains in my own.

My journey felt a great deal like Moses in the wilderness leading the Hebrews from captivity to relative safety. Many of them saw the Promised Land in different ways. When the scouts were sent to check out and came back with the report, only two of them said, "Hey, let's go take them down right now," while the other scouts said, "Oh, no there are some giants over there. We'll be defeated if we go into there." Moses listened to both reports but acted on the one that would fulfill

God's promise. Although he never made it to the Promised Land, his faithful follower, Joshua took the lead and became victorious without even the lift of a sword. The walls of Jericho came tumbling down, and he triumphantly walked the Children of Israel into the Promised Land.

We, too, have the ability to bring down the walls of Jericho in our lives—low self-motivation, lack of opportunity, procrastination, fear—all these things have contributed to the shaky foundation that overpower our very existence.

I also decided to enroll in school again to achieve my Bachelors Degree in Business from DePaul University. I felt empowered and inspired to do all that I could do without FEAR chasing me down. I was elated to complete my Bachelors Degree with a B average. I also started my Masters Degree at the University of Illinois at Chicago and completed my M.A. studies at DePaul University with a 4.0 and was inducted into the Honor Society.

I'm sure that those Biblical warriors—the Children of Israel who walked around the stone walled city seven times, did it in everything from bare feet to sandals. Now women of today can do the same in pumps, mules, stilettos or whatever keeps them jumping over hurdles and challenges.

Step on, ladies. Step on!

Chapter 6: Advice Summary

Now is the time to start doing! Ladies, God is your business partner in your new entrepreneurial endeavor. Don't worry, He has claimed this opportunity and day just for you. Even if you feel a little afraid, do it anyway. Most of your action plan should be written, now let's put some things into action. Incorporate your business, request your tax id (FEIN), write out a clear vision and mission for your business, have someone else review your business plan, understand the financial aspect of your chosen business. Hit the trade shows or go work as an intern within a larger corporation for fine-tuning. It is time to begin your journey of truth . . . the world of entrepreneurship.

Nahum 2:1-2—He who scatters has come up before your face. Man the fort! Watch the road! Strengthen your flanks! Fortify your power mightily. For the LORD will restore the excellence of Jacob Like the excellence of Israel...

CHAPTER 7
STILETTOS
WALKING TALL

My life had taken another major turn. I had made a decision to say NO MORE— no more mental abuse, no more settling for less, no more consistent unhappy days, no more lack of peace. Just the power of simply saying "no more," provides the energy which can help change every single aspect of your life. When you wake up in the morning show your appreciation to God, even before brushing your teeth; show that you are grateful to have breath in your lungs to live that new day. It's a beautiful thing. This new day brings about opportunity . . . an opportunity that you may not have had yesterday.

When mistakes are made, you have an option: you can either bury yourself in the shame or the pain and feel defeated, or you can understand that failure only exists in the grave.

Keep this one statement in mind: "Since I'm still living there's still room for growth, for forgiving myself, forgiving others and building a new me." I am told that cells in the body rejuvenate every seven years which means that on a cellular level, there's a whole new physical you. Now what would happen if there is just a single thought or series of thoughts that transform the mental, emotional and spiritual you? You don't have to wait seven years for that to take place. Why not start in this very moment?

It's just like going out and purchasing a new pair of shoes and putting them on for the first time; it feels so good wearing them, having other people complimenting how they look on your feet—it just feels good. It is the same so it is with taking on a new way of thinking, a thinking that compliments your life and your journey. I realize that I could wake up every single day of my life, and whether I bought a new pair of shoes or not, I could feel so good on the inside. You can, too!

After making God my business partner and speaking positive affirmations over my business, a multitude of good things began to flow. Diamond Bank provided me with a business loan to keep things afloat. Shoe suppliers extended credit (something that had not happened before). The Lord blessed me with an immeasurable company of angels who worked as interns to help lessen my payroll budget. Making God your business partner gains you access to unlimited good. Some things had to be let go, but rebuilding is rejuvenating and doing things God's way instead of your own will lead to life-long prosperity.

An attorney offered to help me on a pro bono basis which extended to the implementation of a song that was developed by myself, Erika Shevon and the Bridge Group managers. Nicole Loftus, a successful business owner who turned her business into a thriving empire, began to mentor me through the Clinton Foundation. In answer to the last item on my vision board, I was filmed for a large network television program. Writing this book was another desire that manifested as well. Miracle…after…miracle…after…miracle.

The conference calls are now comprised of women and men in multiple areas of the United States; all people who are destined to be filled with a daily good word and provided an opportunity to change how they think. Janine, Tiffany and I, along with countless others, are on those calls daily, expecting God's greater good for our lives.

My focus is on complete balance in my life. Learning to enjoy my "me" time, learning to soak my feet in warm water and cuddle up to a nice cozy book instead of a big hard chest (ladies, please know that I'm always for the big hard chest being available when needed, but I'm simply saying don't depend on it). I finally know how to LOVE MYSELF.

These days, I can't wait to see my father and lay a big kiss on him and give him a great big hug. I learned that if he couldn't show me all the love and attention that I needed as a child, I would take that big step and begin living by example. What would happen if I began to show him how to love? He began to show some back! Since I wanted him to hug me, I took the initiative and began to hug him first. Since I wanted him to give me wonderful compliments, I began to compliment him first. What you give out in this world is what you will get in return.

Now we have one of the greatest relationships that a father and daughter could ever have with one another.

My mom is still working on rebuilding her energy, but I believe that she will be fine. Lastly, I'm working on establishing an even closer relationship with my sisters and brothers and sharing what I have learned about love and life. Somehow after my sister's death, even though we got together for birthdays and holidays, pieces of our relationships were stolen. My siblings and I are all working to get it back and build it to be stronger than ever.

I'm walking tall in my stilettos now, feeling stronger than I have ever felt before. I've released the hurt and pain from the past, and taken full responsibility for my own mistakes. I recognize my weaknesses and have the strength to pull myself from those situations or to listen to that still small voice and not to walk into those situations in the first place. I feel revived; I have a new sense of being. I actually feel like I can jump hurdles or even mountains in a single bound. It's not a bird or a plane. No, it's a stiletto-wearing superwoman who knows exactly who she is and what her purpose is in life. Most importantly, she recognizes God is her center.

Won't you slip into a comfortable pair of shoes ... and join me?

Chapter 7: Advice Summary

Walk tall into your new business plan, ladies. Write out your goals for years one through five. Be specific and don't feel as if you can't have big dreams and achieve them. The world belongs to you . . . now embrace it. If you understand that God is your business partner—giving your time, resources and money to the greater good—everything and everyone around you will prosper.

Catherine Ponder quotes, "I am now open and receptive to the rich, divine ideas that now perfectly initiate and sustain my business affairs." Say this affirmation daily.

Give, and it shall be given to you; good measure, pressed down, and shaken together, and running over, shall men give into your bosom. For with the same measure that ye give to others, it shall be measured to you again.
--Webster's Bible Translation of Luke 6:38

"The moment you stop dreaming will feel like the day you stopped breathing."

---Nicole Jones

Please be sure to visit www.daretowalkinmyshoes.com and download a copy of the entreprenuerial worksheet, sign up for the Nicole Jones mailing list, or feel free to share how this book has helped you in some way.

---Nicole Jones

Websites to remember

About the book ...
www.daretowalkinmyshoes.com

Visit my online shoe salon ....
www.sensualstepsinc.com

Learn more about my non-profit organization
www.pumpsuccess.com

Contact me at:
nicole@daretowalkinmyshoes.com

Daily Quotes to Remind Yourself

Nothing in life is for Free…so Work Hard.

Be Afraid, but do it ANYWAY.

When life throws you lemons, don't cry---make lemonade.

Forget about the mistakes of your past, forgive yourself and start from where you are and move forward!

One of the most powerful words in the world to me is stated simply, "Believe."

Speak a positive affirmation to yourself daily, scream out loud if you must…but speak it into existence.

Life is filled with opportunities. Don't let a good one pass you by because of fear.

The moment you stop dreaming will feel like the day you stop breathing.

Failure is only determined once you make it in your grave.

Claim victory for yourself, "Let my unlimited blessings appear now."

Quitting is absolutely not an option.

There will be strife with others, but speak positive existence back into the situation and it will fix itself.

Gossip is for immature women without business…if you are a gossiper get some business quick.

Being negative gets you nowhere fast…slow things down, relax and be positive.

With God you truly can do all things. Trust Him and put your foot down on a matter.

Be proud of who you are and never let others tear your spirits down.

You have options in your life make the right decision

How can you desire a man of your own while you are with someone else's? This is like water and oil . . . it doesn't mix.

As long as you have breath in your lungs to live another day, embrace the unlimited opportunities.

Recommended Reading

Speak it into Existence by Sesvalah
and Naleighna Kai
(www.sesvalah.com) * (www.naleighnakai.com)

The Dynamic Laws of Prosperity
by Catherine C. Ponder

Empowering Women by Louise L. Hay
(www.louisehay.com)

The Writings of Florence Scovel Shinn

You Can Heal Your Life by Louise L. Hay
(www.louisehay.com)

The Art of Extreme Self-Care by Cheryl Richardson
(www.hayhouse.com)

The Law of Attraction 101 by Ehryck F. Gilmore
(www.ehryckgilmore.com)

Remembering Wholeness by Carol Tuttle

Your Best Life Now by Joel Olsten

Ask and it is Given: Learning to Manifest Your Desires
by Ester Hicks, Jerry Hicks and Wayne Dyer

Dancing in the Light by Shirley McClaine

I Quit and Choose Work that Aligns with My Soul
by Karyn Pettigrew

*Women and Money: Owning the Power to Control
Your Destiny* by Suzie Orman

N'DIGO

FREE WEEKLY

A MAGAZINE FOR THE URBANE · DECEMBER 13 - DECEMBER 19, 2007

Nicole Jones:
Sole Queen

abc 7

Shoe Party Today

These shoes will come to you

Bronzeville shop "taking our store on the road"

BY JENNIFER HUNTER

NBC

NBC News Special Feature on Channel 5
with LeeAnn Trotter
Monday, December 3rd, 2007
4:30pm - 5:00pm

CLTV
Chicagoland's
Television

NBC

Sensual Step's Shoe Salon
"Heels on Wheels" Soiree feature on NBC News,
Wednesday, November 29th, 2006

Nicole Jones is the founder of Sensual Steps, Inc., author of *Dare to Walk In My Shoes:* Confessions of A Sole Queen and the owner of NJ Management Company, a property rehabilitation, real estate management and development company. Nicole also hosts monthly seminars and events catered to the growth and development of women, a passion she has harbored for the past fifteen years.

She is known throughout the Midwest region as the "Shoe Professa" or "the Shoe Lady" and has appeared on NBC, ABC, CLTV, WFLD, FOX, The Steve Harvey's Show, and has received spreads in JET and Ebony Magazine, Footwear News Publication and other media outlets.

Nicole is a graduate of DePaul University with a B.A. in Business Management, has also earned the Urban Public Policy Certificate of Graduate Studies at the University of Illinois; and has completed a Master of Arts degree in Applied Professional Studies at Depaul University with a focus on "Urban Studies." In addition, she has received many awards and accolades for community contributions from Breast Cancer Awareness, Weight, Health and Nutrition Programs, Women Finding Internal Peace, Financial Freedom, Prosperity Focus and many other special programs that have helped hundreds of women reach for and obtain a better quality of life.

All the odds were against this young, African American female who grew up on the south side of Chicago with nothing more than integrity and the drive to succeed. Though surrounded by poverty and despair, she refused to settle for less. Armed with the belief that everyone has a preordained purpose, she stepped out on faith to become an "Ordinary Woman, Doing Extraordinary Things."

Nicole is a graduate of Roosevelt University Business Management has also earned the Urban Certificate of Certification Studies at the University and has completed a Master of Arts degree Professional Studies at DePaul University with Urban Studies. In addition, she has received and accolades for community contributions for Awareness, Weight, Health and Nutrition Prog Finding Internal Peace, Financial Freedom, Pos and many other special programs that have been of women reach for and obtain a better quality of

All the odds were against this young female who grew up on the south side of Chicago more than integrity and the drive to succeed. Th by poverty and despair, she refused to settle fo with the belief that everyone has a preordained depend on faith to become an "Ordinary W Extraordinary Things."

LaVergne, TN USA
06 December 2010
207625LV00006B/151/P